WIT, WILL & WALLS

WIT, WILL & WALLS

BY BETTY KILBY FISHER

Pat,

Peace + Blessings

Enjoy

Betty Kilby Fisher

ISBN Paper back: 0-9725709-0-X
UPC: 9780972570909
First Edition
Library of Congress
Card Number: 2002096229

Published by Cultural Innovations, Inc.
P.O. Box 1204
Euless, Texas 76039
Website: www.cultural-innovations.com

Printing by Global Group, Inc.
4901 North Beach Street
Fort Worth, Texas 76137-3498

Printed in the United States of America

⪻ *Wit, Will & Walls* ⪼

"Wit, Will *&* Walls" is the story of little Betty Ann Kilby, an infant plaintiff and her role in the history-making drama of her fight for a high school education. "Wit, Will *&* Walls" is also the story of Betty Ann Kilby Fisher: a powerful woman of God, wife, mother, grandmother and professional woman in her search to find her purpose in life.

❧ Dedicated To ❧

This book is dedicated to my husband, Andrew; my children, Bettina, Renée, Erika, and Tony; my grandchildren, Eric David Jones, Andrew David Owens, Michael Hancock, III, Jeremiah David Gibbs, Derrick Byrd, Gabriel Byrd, Tanesia Fisher, and Tyler Fisher; my parents, Catherine and James Kilby; my sister, Patricia Robb; my brothers, James, John, and Gene; my ancestors, and the victims of the Civil Rights Movement.

❧ *Acknowledgements* ❧

I want to thank my husband, Andrew, who throughout our lives together has been an Officer and a Gentleman. He has always been there to pick me up when I fell allowing me the opportunity to grow and sometimes fail in a warm, supportive and secure environment. He gave me wings and let me fly.

I will always be deeply indebted to my mother for bringing me into this world and for instilling values of honesty, respect, courage and perseverance. I will be forever grateful for my father who with a fourth-grade education accomplished and taught me so much. There would not be a story if it had not been for his vision and his dream.

I want to thank my children, Bettina, Renée, Erika and Tony who have been a source of inspiration, support and love.

I want to give a very special thanks to my friend and my collaborator, Elsa Velazquez.

Introduction

I started to write this book in 1989 when I retired from Rubbermaid. I bought a computer and the "Writer's Guide." I sat for hours as tears flowed from my eyes and a pain in my heart as I recalled the events of my past. I wrote excerpts from the good times in my life but I could not bear to put to paper the painful price of my high school education.

Throughout my life I kept telling God what I wanted, only to find out that he gave me what he wanted me to have. When He took my baby girl through the worst ordeal of my life, I finally gave in to His will and understood that I had to be still and listen to understand that He had a plan, and a purpose for my life.

When I finished chapter three and had put my secret in writing, I couldn't go on. I sat in front of my computer paralyzed; afraid to share my pain and my failures with the world. Like many of my readers, I was brought up believing that there are things that you talk about and there are things that you don't talk about. When I came to understand that my purpose in life was to use my story to educate and encourage others, I had to find the courage to go on. My history is rich with the accomplishments of the African-American people.

We cannot reject the past; nor can we change the past. We must embrace it and take comfort in knowing that the African-American people came through such trials not just once, but over and over again.

This book was written for you to remember all of the people who loved and helped you along the way. It is my desire that as you read this book, you understand that it is not my desire to place blame or to make anyone feel guilty about anything. I wanted to document my story to encourage, educate and motivate you, the reader.

This book should encourage individuals who have not, but must admit, that your problems are greater than you. Find your higher power. Believe in something greater than yourself. Realize that some battles are not yours to fight. Draw yourself so close to that higher power and don't make a step without consulting with Him. Meditate to hear His commands.

❧ Table of Contents ❧

Chapter 1

I AM

I am a child of God, born full of grace, beauty, and dignity!
I am the spirit that will not die!

I was born on February 22, 1945, in Rapidan, Virginia, the third child and first baby girl born to Catherine Elizabeth Ausberry Kilby and James Wilson Kilby. I shared the birthday of the first President of the United States, George Washington. A man who led Americans in battle against British opposition, a man who helped draft the Declaration of Independence and the Constitution of these United States, a man that had deep-rooted beliefs in freedom, yet, a slave owner. It was a day in Virginia, the home of the most eloquent speakers for freedom and equality. It was a state, rich in history and ironies of slavery and freedom.

In accordance with our family tradition, I was dedicated back to God at a Christening ceremony at our home church, Macedonia Baptist Church, during the early months of my life, thus making me a child of God.

I was the third baby in three years. I was delivered by a midwife at the house. Momma almost died having me, she was confined to complete bed-rest for about three weeks. Family friends and neighbors came to help with the housekeeping, cooking and the three children.

At the time of my birth, my father worked on Dr. Eastham's farm in Rapidan, Virginia, by day and in his off-duty hours from the Eastham farm, he was a trapper, farmer and handyman. My mother was the cook, housekeeper, teacher and homemaker.

My Daddy grew up on the Finks farm with his mother and father, Mary Ella Smith Kilby and John Henry Kilby; his three brothers, Charles, Willie and John; and three sisters, Polly, Mildred and Irene. They were considered tenant farmers by Virginia standards; however, their meager existence was a step above slavery. The only difference between their meager existence as tenant farmers and slavery was the fact that the laws had changed and slavery was abolished. Even though my Kilby grandparents were not born into slavery, the slave mentality was born into them.

Most slaves were born free in Africa. They arrived in a strange land after a horrifying journey. They did not speak the language. They were beaten, brutalized, terrorized and victimized until they learned to behave according to the masters will. It was a crime to learn to read or write with a punishment so cruel that many slaves had no interest in learning anything other than the teachings of their master. Even with the Emancipation Proclamation and the 14th Amendment to the Constitution abolishing slavery, many former slaves did not realize that they were free and continued the slave's existence. My Kilby Grandparents must have experienced the suffering of slavery either first-hand or through the stories handed down from generation to generation because they were totally submissive to the Finks. There was very little exposure to the world outside the Finks farm to question their existence until my father came along dreaming the white man's dream of owning his own piece of land.

Mrs. Emma Finks was the mother of Edith and P.M. Finks (old man Dick Finks as my father always referred to him). Miss Emma was a widow ever since my Dad could remember. My grandfather worked for Miss Emma since he was a boy. When Miss Emma died she left the farm to Miss Edith and old man Dick Finks.

My Granddaddy John married my Grandmother, Mary Ella Smith Kilby, (Grandma Ella) and lived on the Finks farm until they died. They had seven children and raised all of their children on the Finks farm. Grandma Ella was a pure-bred Indian. As most Indians in Virginia during that time period, her family lived in the mountains and were often referred to as "Mountain People." My grandmother, died from a brain hemorrhage just sixteen days after I was born. Daddy really took Grandma Ella's death hard. He could not let go of the feeling and the reality that the Finks had simply worked her to death. Although, I didn't know her up-close and personal, momma and daddy made sure that I knew her from their stories. Daddy told me that I looked a lot like Grandma Ella, with her fair skin and petite form. They said that I also had a warm, loving and sensitive nature like Grandma Ella.

My Granddaddy John (John Henry Kilby) died while out in the field when he was seventy-two-years old. During one of our Sunday visits to Peola Mills, Granddaddy John was sick, however old man Dick Finks (the master of the Finks farm) did not acknowledge that Granddaddy John was sick, therefore, Granddaddy John did not acknowledge that he was sick and continued performing his work in the field.

When we got home from our visit, Daddy called one of his white friends for help. The next day Daddy, his white friend and our family doctor went back to Peola Mills to visit Granddaddy John. The doctor diagnosed my Granddaddy as having pneumonia, and they tried to convince him to go to the hospital. Because Daddy's friend was a white man he tried to reason with old man Dick Finks to encourage Granddaddy to go to the hospital. All efforts failed. The doctor left some medicine, but Granddaddy died three days later. When they found Granddaddy, he was in the field sitting under the cow with a half-a-bucket of milk and his hands molded around the cow's utters.

The day after Granddaddy John's death we got the news that Aunt Mary's (Momma's oldest sister) oldest daughter Arvelon (Fee) had died in a fire. Fee had four little children and she was pregnant with the fifth when she died. Fee was burned so badly the baby inside her was also burned around the lips, eyes and nose. It was the tradition for the family to get together at the home of the deceased to comfort the bereaving family; therefore, we made the journey across the mountain to Flint Hill to the Roberts' home. The grown folks sat around talking about the accident. We saw the burned bush where Fee had come to her untimely end. Her youngest toddler was burned on his forehead because he was holding on to his momma's dress tail as she ran outside in a blaze. Fee and her newborn baby were buried on Sunday afternoon. We left Fee's funeral and went to Culpepper for family night. Granddaddy John was buried on Monday. There was so much sadness in our home during that week. I couldn't pinpoint the greatest source of pain and agony. I couldn't determine if Daddy mourned for my beautiful, young cousin and her kids or his father who had aroused so much internal agony and anguish.

When Grandma Ella's first son Charles was born, he was given to the Finks to raise in the big house as though he was white. Old man Dick Finks and his sister Edith Mae Finks inherited the farm and worked the farm together. To the general public Charles was Miss Edith's nigger. To Daddy, Charles was another pawn of slavery. Uncle Charles didn't work the farm like my Daddy. He had good clothes, ate the same foods as the Finks, he went to school and was trained to be a carpenter and furniture maker. When Uncle Charles died he was buried in Fairview Cemetery alongside the Finks. Daddy grew up confused and angry when he compared his lifestyle to the lifestyle of his older brother Charles.

Daddy was confused by and upset with Charles's relationship with the Finks. Daddy served Charles just like he served the Finks. He especially hated to empty the pots Charles and the Finks used for urinating and defecating. Sometimes, Charles would go in the pot and make Daddy clean his pot just for spite because he knew how much Daddy hated that task. Daddy had a love-hate relationship with Uncle Charles that ate away at him. He often blamed his dark skin for being treated different.

I grew up believing that my Granddaddy John was not Uncle Charles's father. I believed that old man Dick Finks was Charles's father. I think that my Daddy thought so too, but it was one of those subjects that we were not allowed to talk about. My Daddy loved his mother so much he would not accept that she had laid with old man Dick Finks.

I wondered if my Grandma Ella's body was taken during the day, perhaps while Granddaddy John worked the fields or did old man Dick Finks call for my Grandma at night like the old masters in the slave movies. Did she fight? Or did she just give in to old man Dick Finks as if it were part of her duties as a house nigger? Granddaddy John and Uncle Charles appeared to have a closer relationship than Daddy and Granddaddy.

When old man Dick Finks died, he left all of his worldly goods to Charles and my cousin Russell. Aunt Polly conceived and had a baby (Russell), out of wedlock while living and working on the Finks farm. I imagined and wondered if old man Dick Finks took my aunt in the same manner that he took my Grandma. When Aunt Polly got married and left the Finks farm she did not take her son Russell with her. Why would she leave her son? Why did old man Dick Finks let him stay? Like Uncle Charles, he had more white features than colored features. It was another one of those things that we were not allowed to talk about. But, yes, I believed that old man Dick Finks, a man, no, a monster laid with both Granddaddy John's wife and Granddaddy's daughter. They could stop me from talking but they couldn't stop me from thinking. Russell inherited the Finks farm when Uncle Charles died.

I can imagine the pain and agony that my father suffered. As a child, I thought the battle was in Daddy's mind and that it was a love-hate relationship over the difference in the fact that Uncle Charles was treated with dignity and respect while my Daddy was treated more like a slave. The vein ran deeper than what one could determine on the surface.

In moments of weakness and despair, Daddy talked about his being black and compared his blackness to evil as the destructive black birds and the black cat. However, no sooner the ugly words of his blackness were spoken, he would compose himself and talk about how our African ances-tors were Kings and Queens and how they were snatched from their home land, and boarded on the ship like animals. He would say "evil, evil, I'll tell you what's evil, robbing a man of his dignity is evil, violating my momma and my sister is evil, killing my momma is evil, old man Dick Finks is evil, I am not evil with my black skin, I am born to be great because God created me black." He would lecture us and tell us to look in the mirror and say, "I am a child of God, born full of grace, beauty and dignity, the world didn't give me this grace, beauty and dignity and the world can't take it away from me." At the mention of God, he would say hate the sin and love the sinner. After hearing all the stories about old man Dick Finks, it was hard for me as a child to separate the sin from the sinner.

Daddy had lived and worked on the Finks farm all his life and when he was seventeen, he threatened to leave. November 1936, old man Dick Finks gave Daddy the deed to 24 acres of land with a run-down shack to entice Daddy to stay and continue to work on the farm. Finks also promised to pay Daddy six dollars per month for his labor. Daddy always wanted to be a landowner and he believed that the land and labor was the key to economic prosperity just as land and slave labor was the key to prosperity for the early settlers of Virginia. What Daddy didn't realize was that he could not afford the start-up expenses to renovate the run-down shack and clear, seed and cultivate his land. After old man Dick Finks charged Daddy room and board, there was nothing left from his wages to pursue his dream. More often than not, he ended up owing old man Dick Finks. Since no money changed hands, there was no written statement of wages, and with Daddy's limited education, Daddy couldn't determine if he was cheated or not. The one thing he was sure of was that he owned 24 acres of land because he had legal papers. After nearly five more years of working on the Finks farm from sunrise to sunset, he realized that when old man Dick Finks got through working him like a slave, there was no time, money, energy or vision to cultivate his land. There was no one with business expertise to tell him what to do. Daddy lost sight of working his 24 acres and decided to set his sights on a more realistic goal.

He decided that having a car was more advantageous and more attain-able, besides he could earn extra money by setting traps and selling furs while performing his duties on the Finks farm and no one would be the wiser. When Daddy earned enough money from his furrier business he purchased his first car, a 1933 maroon Chevrolet for $150. Daddy taught us that sometimes you have to re-evaluate your priorities and sometimes you just need to have a little fun.

With that car, Daddy found my Momma. Daddy also found a way to turn the car into a business enterprise. He worked on the Finks farm Monday through Saturday and oftentimes on Sunday. When Daddy was off work detail on Saturday nights and Sundays, he was making engagements to taxi the school teachers to various local functions. One Saturday night, he was commissioned to carry a couple of teachers to the Miss Rappahannock Contest at the Flint Hill Elementary School. While on this trip to Flint Hill, Daddy met my Momma. Momma was crowned Miss Rappahannock. Momma won the contest based on the fact that she raised the highest amount of money to donate to the school district, $14. According to Daddy, Momma was a vision of beauty and loveliness. For Daddy it was love at first sight. Even though Daddy was very much in love with Momma, he thought he could have his cake and eat it too. On a particular Friday night, Momma went to church in Sperryville, Virginia. Daddy suspected that Momma may come to this particular church on this particular Friday night, however, just in case she couldn't make it to church, Daddy brought his old girl friend Maybelle. Daddy commissioned his baby brother, my Uncle John to be the look out. Uncle John was supposed to warn Daddy when he saw Momma. Uncle John saw Momma; he was so taken with her beauty that he forgot his post and he forgot about his job of letting Daddy know that Momma made it to the church. Daddy was busted! According to Momma, her brother made up a song and sang all the way back to Flint Hill, "more little yellow girls than one, old Kilby was gonna have some fun with more little yellow girls than one." Daddy lead us to believe that Momma was okay with his two-timing, playboy attitude, however, shortly after that Momma and Daddy got married.

On Saturday April 19, 1941, Daddy got up early that morning, did his day's work digging and harvesting potatoes and got married at three that afternoon. I believe that Daddy had to ask my Momma to marry him because he feared losing her. Daddy's plan for the happy ever after was weak and did not match his usual well-planned ideas. Daddy had the nerve to take my Momma back to the Finks farm with him. Miss Edith Finks (old man Dick Finks' sister and partner in running the Finks farm) certainly had plans for Momma. Miss Edith had plans for my Momma to work in the kitchen on one of the neighboring farms. I can see the thought flash through Daddy's head of my Momma being violated by the master of the house just like his momma and his sister.

Momma must have really been in love with my Daddy to go to the Finks farm with Daddy in the first place. She was much too spirited to be a house nigger. She had not been exposed to having to work outside the home. Daddy took Momma back to Flint Hill to live with her family until he could come up with a better plan. The Ausberry family welcomed my Daddy into the family with love and joy.

Momma was the eighth child born to Sarah Elizabeth Jordan Ausberry and Frank Ausberry (Granddaddy Frank). The Ausberry family shed all symbols of slavery. They gave up their slave name and decided to be Ausberrys, however everyone had a different view on how that name should be spelled, from census records, legal documents to individual family members. Uncle Raymond, the eldest son, spelled his name Allsburry, Uncles James, John, Jordan, Carter and Robert spelled their names as Alsberry. According to Momma after completing the seventh grade she kept on walking the six miles to school for the next three to four years. Momma got so smart that one day while studying phonics, she decided that the family name was misspelled. She decided that the correct spelling of her name should be Ausberry. My momma, Aunt Mary and Uncle Edgar all spelled their name Ausberry.

Unlike my Kilby Grandparents who could not rise above slavery, my Ausberry Grandparents were able to pull themselves up out of the pits of slavery to prosperity. Granddaddy Frank learned how to play the game very early in life. He walked around with a gunny sack on his back collecting bottles and things that other people threw away. He would walk into Bradford's store and ask, "what you got for a good ole niggar?" Daddy hated the use of the term "Nigger" that was the slang and derogatory title used for Negroes. The white folks liked it when Granddaddy Frank referred to himself as a good old niggar. Granddaddy Frank explained the difference in niggar and niggar. He used the term "Niggar" and referred to himself as a stingy person and he surely was a stingy person. The white folks interpreted the word as Nigger, because of their interpretation he could hang out at Bradford's store for hours listening as the white men talked about business. He listened, learned and emulated those businessmen. He would say, "The wise old owl sat in an oak. The more he saw the less he spoke. The less he spoke, the more her heard. We should all be like that bird."

By the colored standard in those days, Granddaddy Frank was considered a rich Negro. He had two buggies, one with a fancy cover for Sundays and one without a cover. He was the first black man in Rappahannock to buy a car, a black Model A Ford. When Granddaddy Frank got sick and had to have back surgery in March of 1925, he went to Winchester Memorial Hospital. He paid $24.00 for his five-day stay, $10.00 for the operating room fee, $5.00 for anesthetic, $3.00 for lab work and twenty cents for the phone call that indicated that he had a phone as early as 1925.

Granddaddy Frank was the local veterinarian. He did not have any formal training. According to Momma, Granddaddy Frank followed the local veterinarian around and became a self-taught veterinarian. In the later years, when Granddaddy Frank went to neighboring farms to tend to the animals, he would take Momma along to handle the money. Now, Granddaddy Frank was no dummy when it came to handling money, he bought Road Bonds and invested his money in land and rental property. He owned 200 acres of farmland with an apple and peach orchard. In addition to working on the farm, his sons picked apples and peaches. Granddaddy Frank sold the unblemished fruit. The family used the blemished fruit for canning, preserves and consumption. When the boys grew up and left the farm, Granddaddy Frank rented out the orchard.

Momma was no stranger to hard work. The girls tended the chickens, picked berries, harvested and preserved the fruits and vegetables. They cooked and cleaned the house. Granddaddy Frank raised mostly beef cattle, however, he did have a couple of milk cows to provide milk for the family. Momma and Aunt Mary were also responsible for milking the cows. During his lifetime, Granddaddy Frank amassed a 350-acre estate and a net worth of over $100,000 that was considered a fortune in those days.

During the late 1880's through the 1950's, many colored farms and homes were burned if the white people perceived that the colored's were becoming too prosperous. Granddaddy Frank was one of the lucky ones.

Granddaddy Frank was the epitome of economical thrift. He had money in three banks; he had so much money that he buried it in jars on the property. There were stories of the new owners finding thousands of dollars buried in jars when his estate was sold. He became senile in his old age.

When Granddaddy Frank's sons worked away from the farm and were paid wages, Granddaddy Frank took their earnings and would give them a dollar. The boys would send Momma to negotiate on their behalf, they told

Momma to ask for two dollars for their allowance instead of the usual dollar. Momma was successful in getting the boys more money most of the time. As each son turned eighteen, Granddaddy Frank offered them a thousand dollars and a piece of land to build their house. If they refused that offer, they got five hundred dollars to start their lives on their own.

Uncle Raymond bought a piece of land in Amissville, Virginia, about ten miles from the home place in Rappahannock County. Uncle James moved to Pennsylvania, Uncle Robert bought a piece of land in Freetown (Free Negro settlement outside of Flint Hill), Uncle Jordan, Carter, John and Edgar bought land in Strasburg (ten miles west of Front Royal). Granddaddy Frank set a good example and all of his sons owned land and bought their own homes. The girls, even though they worked on the farm too, they were not so amply rewarded. They inherited the vision of owning land and their husbands provided homes for them.

When we ask Granddaddy Frank when was he born, he would say, "second Sunday in February." For many years we celebrated his birthday on the second Sunday in February. Upon his death, we found an envelope with a note that said, "Frank Alsberry born February 10, 1881, son of Diana Beasley and Shelton Williams Allsberry; married to Sarah Elizabeth Jordan on March 29, 1902."

We could not find any records documenting Grandma Sarah's birthday. The family Bible had a notation that she was born in 1882 and died in 1944 and that she had taken ill the first Sunday in January 1934. My Momma told me that Grandma had a stroke. The stroke left her with nerve damage to her left arm, but it didn't stop her from riding the horse six miles to Freetown to have wine and cake with her friends. Momma said Grandma was a high-spirited woman.

According to Mamma, Grandma Sarah wanted for sometime to visit her family in West Virginia. Granddaddy Frank finally drove her to West Virginia to visit her family. When she got to her family's home and saw her family, she got so excited; she had a heart attack and died before she got to the house. She was buried in the family cemetery on the property near the apple orchard alongside her two babies that died shortly after they were born.

Granddaddy Frank was not a religious man, however three of his sons grew up to be preachers. It had to be from Grandma's teachings. We found receipts where Grandma Sarah bought religious material through the mail. Granddaddy Frank only went to church once a year on homecoming Sunday (third Sunday in July). On homecoming Sunday, there were two services.

Before our church (Macedonia Baptist Church) built a dining room onto the church, the men would build temporary tables along side the road entering into the church property. The women would drape white muslin material over the tables. Each church family bought food, country ham, fried chicken, string beans with ham hocks, macaroni and cheese, corn pudding, lemon meringue pie, pound cake, yeast rolls and corn bread. Food was in abundance on homecoming Sunday. People came from far and near. Some of the people, like my Granddaddy Frank came, ate lunch and went home. The church was so full that chairs were put in the aisles. There was no way that all the people could get into the church for evening service, therefore, a loud speaker was set-up so that people on the outside could hear the service. The children were allowed to stay outside and socialize with the many family and friends. Parents didn't worry since any adult could correct any child misbehaving. Daddy usually managed one of the selling stands that sold soda pop, candy, ice cream and sandwiches. He kept a watchful eye on us.

The time had come for Momma and Daddy to move out on their own. When they put their heads together they came up with a plan for being together. Momma collected and sold rat-tails and she took in ironing to generate a little bit of spare money. Daddy continued his furrier business. Daddy finally left the Finks farm in 1942. Nearly six years after receiving his 24 acres of land, Daddy still could not afford to cultivate or make a home on his place. Even then, old man Dick Finks threatened to turn Daddy into the Army Board. Daddy got a job working on Dr. Eastham's farm. He sold his car, rented a house, bought a stove, a radio and a cow. The yearlong commute was over and the newly weds were together at last.

The honeymoon didn't last long. My brother James was born April 13, 1942 (on Thomas Jefferson's birthday), just sixteen months later on August 1, 1943, my brother John was born. My brother John is just eighteen months older than me.

One day when one of the neighbors was at the house helping my Momma while she was recuperating from having me, my brothers James (Jimmy) and John (Bubble) decided that they wanted some candy. They worked all day trying to catch a chicken to take to the country store to trade for some candy. Not able to catch the chicken, they noticed two eggs in the nest. They took the eggs to the country store and traded the eggs for some candy. That evening when Daddy got off from work, the storekeeper called him into the store and handed the two eggs to my Daddy. He told Daddy that Jimmy and Bubble traded the eggs for some penny candy. They both laugh when the storekeeper said, "Hey Wilson, chips off the old block eh?" After dinner Daddy called the boys and he placed Jimmy on one knee and Bubble on the other knee. He explained that they took the eggs that were not theirs to take. He used this opportunity to teach a lesson on honesty. When Daddy told this story, he told it with such pride, it was easy to determine that he was quite proud of his sons and their ability to get what they wanted and to know that they were emulating what they saw him doing. It was no small wonder that they would imitate Daddy since he carried the boys everywhere with him. He would carry the boys with him when he went to check his traps. According to Momma, it was nothing to see Daddy walking across the field with the two boys on his back and his booty from his traps in a gunny sack tied around his waist dragging along behind him. With a wife and three kids, Daddy did all kinds of extra jobs to care for his family.

One of Daddy's many part-time jobs was running turkeys from Rapidan to Front Royal, an approximately forty-mile journey. They did not ride horses; they walked the turkeys. Daddy would say, "domestic turkeys are so dumb that you have to teach them how to eat or they would starve to death, when it rains you have to herd them to shelter or they would hold their beaks up in the air until they drown." When I see the cowboys in the cowboy movies herding the cows and horses to market, I think about my Daddy running turkeys.

It was on one of these trips to Front Royal that convinced Daddy that Front Royal was a good place to work and raise his family. Besides, he had heard so much about Front Royal from my Ausberry uncles. Four of my mother's brothers and her brother-in-law worked at the American Viscose Plant in Front Royal, over in Warren County about twenty miles north of Flint Hill, Virginia. This job had afforded them an opportunity to buy their homes. They suggested to Daddy that he, too, should apply for a job at the Viscose.

Being a part of the Ausberry family exposed Daddy to a very different lifestyle. They showed Daddy that all those things that he dreamed about were possible and attainable. Daddy got a job at the American Viscose Plant too. Daddy rented a house in Happy Creek three miles east of Front Royal at the foot of the horseshoe that made-up the Happy Creek colored community. Daddy had great expectations from this community of Happy Creek. He said, "only happiness can come from Happy Creek, I liked the sound of Happy Creek as it rolled off my tongue, Happy Creek, Happy Creek." Daddy had to move to the country where he could have room for his cow and chickens. Shortly after moving to Happy Creek, my sister, Patricia, was born on St. Patrick's Day, March, 17, 1948. Pat was the first of the Kilby children to be born in a hospital. Daddy had great expectations for Pat too because she was born on the luckiest day of the year. Daddy learned that "Kilby" was an Irish name. He would say, "with an Irish name, we have to believe in the luck of the Irish."

It wasn't long before Daddy became part of the Happy Creek connection. Happy Creek was a small Negro community where most of the Negro residents owned their land and operated small farms. Many of the large jobs were a community effort. When the Baltimores killed hogs, the entire neighborhood was there to help with the process; men, women and children. At one time, the Starks owned the only tractor in the neighborhood. When the job called for a tractor, Mr. Starks and his tractor was there to lend a helping hand. Most of the communities' social activity centered around a large project.

I especially remember the apple butter party. Apple butter is a product cooked until it is brown and the consistency of thick sweet applesauce. It is best when cooked outside in an iron kettle on the open fire. It is used like jam and jellies.

Harry F. Byrd, a well-known politician owned an apple orchard in Berryville, Virginia. Every year after he had harvested the apples, he would invite the local community to come to his orchard to pick the sub-standard apples that were left on the tree and apples that had fallen to the ground. Many Happy Creek residents would go and pick apples from Byrd's orchard. More often that not, the Kilby's got their apples from Granddaddy Franks orchard. Each family would contribute something to the party. If a family didn't bring apples, they would bring sugar or jars for storing the apple butter. The ladies assessed the need for apple butter from of each participating family. They also solicited from each family until they had sufficient materials to make enough apple butter to satisfy the needs of each family. Everyone in the community brought something for the potluck dinner. The ladies and children of the community gathered early on Saturday morning and split into work groups. With the week-long planning, everyone knew his or her work assignments. Everyone worked including the children, but this work was fun. The men would gather throughout the day, but they were definitely there in time for dinner. There was always a minister in the midst to bless the food for dinner as well as bless the occasion and the apple butter. We generally ate outside on make shift tables that were used at each party.

One work group was in charge of processing the apples, while another work group was in charge of getting the fire started and keeping the fire going under the black pots. Another group was responsible for cooking and stirring the mixture to keep the apple butter from sticking. And another group was responsible for canning the final product. On Sunday after church, the community got together again for distribution of the apple butter to the participating families. Anyone in the neighborhood who could not participate because they were too old or incapacitated would receive ample apple butter to last until the next apple butter party.

Happy Creek had two churches, Mt. Nebo and St. Paul, both were Baptist, however, they belonged to different associations; one was old-school Baptist and the other was new-school Baptist. Even though the Kilbys were members of Macedonia Baptist Church in Flint Hill, we were active in both churches in Happy Creek as well. We usually attended Sunday school and church at St. Paul on second and fourth Sundays and Mt. Nebo Sunday school on first and third Sundays. On third Sundays Daddy would pick us up early from Sunday school and we would go to the Macedonia church in Flint Hill. Daddy would take us kids to Sunday school every Sunday morning. Then he would go back home and get dressed for church. Depending on the Sunday, Daddy and Momma would come back to St. Paul or Mt. Nebo for the eleven o'clock morning church service. Our whole social life revolved around the church and family setting.

When we went to Macedonia church in Flint Hill, Daddy would stop in town (Front Royal) and put gas in the car and also get a loaf of bread. By the time we got out of church, us children would be starving. The car smelled like a bakery, which made us even hungrier. The four of us made a pact. If we opened the loaf of bread, we would have to eat the whole loaf; every one had to swear to keep their mouths shut and we all had to convince Daddy that he did not buy bread at the gas station. We ate the whole loaf, threw the bag in the trash at church, opened the car windows and sprayed perfume in the car so that Daddy would be convinced that he didn't buy bread that Sunday. Most of the time we got away with it, especially when we were going to visit our relatives in Woodville, Slate Mills or Peola Mills, Virginia.

Daddy would say these relatives are poor, if they ask you if you are hungry say, "no thank you." We made sure that we repeated the words as instructed. We also made sure that our aunts could read our pitiful faces. Aunt Mildred and Aunt Irene always cooked-up a big meal on Sunday and they always had a big pound cake either in the oven or available for guest. They would say, "we know our brother, we gonna eat today and ya'll eat a plenty." The children would play outside while the grownups visited.

On this particular Sunday we were playing this circle game. It went like this: we would join hands, get in a circle and sing "up the green mountain, down the green hill, the last one squat gonna tell their will." If you were the last one to squat, you had to tell a secret or something that all the other players didn't know. When I got caught, I began to sing, "old man Dick Finks stole my Daddy's land, old man Dick Finks stole my Daddy's land." Daddy was somewhere lurking out of sight. He heard me. He came from out of nowhere. He yanked me up by the arm and he wore my butt out unmercifully. The veins in his forehead looked like they were about to pop and he rolled his tongue up and you could see the veins under his tongue. He made me sit in the car until he was ready to leave while everyone else ate dinner and cake. That night we rode home in silence. I was a grown woman before I understood why I took that terrible beating that day.

The church members would host events such as, box socials, rummage sales and Tom Thumb weddings. At the box socials, the girls and women would make dinners and wrap the dinner in fancy wrappings. The moderator would read off the contents of the box dinner, however the person that prepared dinner was a secret. The men would bid on the box dinners and would share the dinner with the person who prepared the feast. It was so much fun watching the bidding and the surprise expressions when the bidder found out who they were going to be sharing their box dinner with.

The Tom Thumb wedding was a mock wedding with children characters. I was the bride in the Tom Thumb wedding when I was six years old. Ezekiel Baltimore was the groom. Ezekiel and I told people that we were married. When we grew up we went on a date, we discovered that the fantasy of our youth should be preserved in the past.

Rev. James Phillip Baltimore approached Daddy at one of the social functions and told Daddy that he had 100 acres of land to sell for $10,500. Rev. Baltimore was not interested in farming. He ran the local grocery store, had a radio ministry and was the pastor of several local churches. Daddy did not have enough money saved to buy all 100 acres. Rev. Baltimore wanted to sell the 100 acres as a package. Daddy approached two of his buddies at work about going in together and buying the land. Ruben Barbour had a wife and home in the town of Front Royal, however, he was interested in farming. He also had ties in Happy Creek because he was a member of Mt. Nebo Baptist Church and the superintendent of the Sunday school at Mt. Nebo. Thorl Jackson lived in Howardsville, Virginia, with his wife and a little boy that they were raising. Howardsville was about fifteen miles from the Viscose down in the mountain with dirt roads more than half of the distance. It was a rough commute to work. Both of these guys decided that they wanted a piece of this action. Daddy got 52 acres, Mr. Barbour got 20 acres and Bro Thorl got 28 acres.

I knew something was up because Aunt Alice came to the house to take care of us while Momma and Daddy went to close on the land. Aunt Alice was not a blood relative. In the small community of Happy Creek, it was not unusual to address close loved ones as aunt or uncle. When Momma and Daddy returned home, we all packed into the old truck and drove over to our land. My Daddy jumped out of the truck, ran, fell down and rolled around kicking his feet all the time saying "thank you Jesus, thank you Jesus, thank you, thank you, thank you, thank you, this is my land." Finally, Momma said, "you crazy man come on here, you are scaring the kids." Daddy got up. He came over to the truck, picked up Momma and sat her on the back of the truck, then he picked up all of us kids one by one and sat us on the back of the truck. He paced back and forth in front of us with this big smile on his face. He said, "this is our land, this is our land, we are going to work this land and reap the profits from this land. The house will go over there. The barn will be down there. We are going to have milking cows and we are going to sell milk. We are going to have chickens and we are going to sell eggs. Oh, we need a chicken house, so we will put the chicken house over there and we will build the outhouse beside the chicken house. We need some pigs and a meat house to store the meat when we butcher. We have to put the meat house close to the house. We are going to grow fruit and vegetables, cherries, apples, peaches, tomatoes, potatoes, corn and beans. My dreams are coming true, at last, I see."

Everyday Daddy would go to work at the Viscose, come home, eat dinner and head over to our land on the other side of the tracks. Momma taught the boys how to milk the cow and we would collect the eggs and tend the chickens and clean up the kitchen. Every Saturday we would go over to the property to work. The neighbors helped too. At last we were ready to move.

Daddy built a three-bedroom brick home, an outside toilet, a chicken coop and barn with four stalls so that he could milk the cows inside. We moved in on a Wednesday. Daddy was so anxious to get the yard squared away that he was out in the dark with the lights on the tractor tilling and grading the yard so that he could plant grass seed. I sat on the steps with the front door open watching the tractor lights going up and down the yard. Finally, Momma went outside and made Daddy put the tractor away. When Daddy came into the house he realized that he had lost his wallet in the yard. He had stopped and cashed his pay check for the week before he came home that evening. He had his week's pay in that wallet. We gathered all of the flashlights we could find. Daddy set the tractor with the lights on moving the tractor from section to section until we had carefully checked each section inch-by-inch. Again Momma interceded and called an end to the search. I can hear Daddy now bargaining with God, "God, I am doing the very best that I can to support my family and raising my children under your covenant, please help me find my wallet." The next morning Momma got up early and went out in the yard again combing through the earth. She came back in the house yelling, "thank you Jesus, I found it, I found it."

Daddy said, "now we needed some animals." Daddy read about the 4-H Club in the newspaper. There weren't any colored 4-H Clubs in Front Royal. He talked with Chuck Leadman, Business Manager for the Union and suggested that the Union sponsor the 4-H Club for the colored children. Chuck Leadman got the Lions Club to co-sponsor the project along with TWUA Local 371. In late April of 1953, Daddy organized the Colored 4-H Club Adult Council. He was elected President. The other officers were: Charles Baltimore, Vice President; Sam Fletcher, Secretary; Ruben Barbour, Treasurer; and Rev. Baltimore, Chaplain. The newly organized 4-H Club assembled at our house on Monday, May 4, 1953 to receive 14 pigs to be raised by the colored boys and girls of the club. This was the first time that Daddy allowed us to play with the animals. He used to say, "farm animals are for feeding and working, if you understand that now, there won't be no crying at slaughtering time." Jimmy and Bubble named their hogs Sadie and Sally. Sadie and Sally were kept separate from the other hogs. Both Jimmy and Bubble raised prize-winning hogs at the fair that year. Daddy used their hogs for breeding and Jimmy and Bubble got one baby pig from each litter. If they decided to sell their pig, they would get the proceeds from the sale. Daddy would make them put the money in the bank.

He would say, "I'm teaching you responsibility and business because I can't leave it for you to learn in school, it's too important."

I would get mad because I had to do the work in the house. I didn't get any proceeds from washing those dirty old milk buckets or raising the chickens. When I raised the issue, Daddy would say, "you are a girl and girls do the light work and the house work that don't generate a profit." As I got older, I figured out how a girl could get paid. I learned to bake. As Daddy bragged about his little girl's cooking to his buddies at work, I began to pack an extra piece of cake for Deacon Mosie or Deacon Brooks. I got request for cakes and sold them to Daddy's friends. I reminded Daddy that I could also generate a profit. We figured that the ingredients cost one dollar. I sold the cake for five dollars. I got to keep four dollars every time I sold a cake.

Every spring the local feed store, Southern States ran a special. With every twenty-five pounds of chicken feed that you purchase, you would get twenty-five baby chicks. We would get no less than seventy-five to one hundred baby chicks during the month-long sale. In anticipation of the arrival of the baby chicks, Daddy would stop by the local furniture store and get large cardboard boxes and set them up in the basement. We had a big light that hung about six inches over the baby chicks to keep them warm. Daddy bought special tops that we screwed onto half-gallon jars to put water in for the chicks. When you turned the jars of water up-side-down, the water would come down and fill the trays. We used old half-gallon mason jars that had chips along the top edge. These jars couldn't be used for canning. We put feed in the saucers that had cracks and chips. It was Momma's responsibility to raise the baby chicks. The mortality rate among the baby chicks was very high. If we were lucky approximately half of the chickens would make it to the frying and laying stage.

By the time I reached my seventh birthday, I could wring the chicken's neck and pluck the feathers. As I got older, I was able to chop off the chicken's head and dip it in boiling water. We would kill a minimum of three chickens every Saturday. Momma would stew the chicken feet, heart, neck and gizzards for Saturday's dinner. She would boil them in a pot and make milk gravy. I didn't like this meal because you could see the black pepper floating in the white gravy. I thought the pepper was dirt from the chickens' feet. Daddy didn't make me eat this meal for fear that I would waste good food. The chicken feet mixture was served over biscuits. I would make a meal of biscuits and jelly. Momma fried the chicken livers for Sunday's breakfast and served them with some fried potatoes, eggs and hot rolls. No sooner than we were finished with breakfast Momma started frying the chickens for dinner. Leftovers were used for our lunches on Monday.

Daddy reminded us how lucky we were. He told us that growing up, on the Finks farm, he rarely got to eat any of the good parts of the chicken. Daddy said that he ate so many necks and backs growing up "I don't ever want to see another chicken back on my table, nothing but the best for my children." He would have Momma split the chicken down the back with half the back attached to the thigh and the other half of the back attached to the breast portion and she threw the neck in Saturday night's gravy. Dad's other saying was "waste not want not." We were required to eat everything on our plates. Daddy drilled that saying in us so hard it is another one of those rules that I will never forget.

Every time Daddy got a little money saved, he bought another cow or a pig. Every Monday was stock sale day; Daddy would go to the sale when he got off work looking for bargains. Granddaddy Frank also attended the sales. He went around saying "what you got for a good ole niggar today?" The operators at the stockyard would give Granddaddy Frank the sick animals or animals that they could not sell, like a calf that would not survive without its mother but too young and weak to butcher. Granddaddy would nurse the sick animal to good health, sell it and make a profit. The "good ole niggar" routine worked and it was profitable. Even with the understanding of Granddaddy's "Niggar" analogy, Daddy was embarrassed, however the time that Granddaddy Frank gave Momma a malnourished calf that he got free at the stockyard, Daddy didn't complain. Daddy respected Granddaddy Frank's knowledge of animals and his ability to negotiate a deal. Daddy blamed his purchase of a hog or a cow or a calf on Granddaddy Frank to keep Momma from getting mad. If Daddy bought Granddaddy home for dinner on a particular Monday, we knew that there was surely a new animal in the barnyard. Any other day of the week would mean one of the cows was ready to deliver a new calf or one of the animals was sick.

With Momma expecting another baby, no matter how creative Daddy was in stuffing two adults and four children into the truck, he couldn't figure out how to get another baby into the truck. For the next nine months, Daddy concentrated on saving money for a car. Daddy carried Momma to the hospital in the truck and he bought her home in our new car. Daddy paid cash for the car using his savings and the profit from the sale of some live-stock. Daddy bought a second hand car from someone at work and he kept the truck. Daddy said, "You can't have a farm without a truck."

By the time my brother Gene arrived on October 28, 1951, the yard was beautifully landscaped with box bushes on each side of the front porch. We had two rows of fruit trees with a variety of apple, cherry and peach trees. Most people had cherry trees that produced red or black cherries; we had a cherry tree that produced yellow cherries. We canned the red and black cherries. There were never enough yellow cherries to can because Daddy would brag about his yellow cherry tree and he had to show his buddies at work his yellow cherries. We also ate these cherries to our hearts content. Momma made the best cherry pies and cobblers with the red and black cherries. When the apples, cherries and peaches were in season, we ate fruit until we were sick. We processed, and canned the fruit for the winter, never wasting anything. We did the same thing with the garden vegetables. Sometimes there was so much food; we would share with the neighbors. The work seemed to be never ending. We grew practically everything we ate.

When we thrashed wheat, we would keep a portion of the wheat and have the wheat ground into flour for breads, pastries and gravies. When we grew corn, besides eating corn-on-the-cob, canning corn and storing corn for feeding the cows, chickens and hogs during the winter, we would have a portion of the corn ground into cornmeal for corn bread. The chickens produced eggs that we exchanged at the local grocery store for coffee, sugar and a few other things that we could not grow on the farm. We butchered at least one hog and one cow every year.

We learned in school that Virginia had only one growing season. Wrong! As soon as we completed the spring, summer and fall harvest, Daddy planted turnips and greens. The good news about the winter harvest is that we didn't can the turnips or the greens. The bad news was that it was cold, wet and damp harvesting turnips, greens and field cress in the winter. The winter was as harsh as the humid heat of the summer.

Daddy would check the almanac and weather reports because once the temperature dropped to freezing, it was hog killing time. Thanksgiving was the most ideal time for butchering hogs because of the extra days off from work. Sometimes the tripods for hanging the pigs would be set-up for weeks waiting for the weather to get cold enough to butcher. Momma's brother, my Uncle Robert T, had the most experience at butchering and he had three or four grown sons, therefore, the event had to be planned around his schedule. This event required at least five or six strong men the first night of the butchering usually on Friday night. Uncle Robert T and sometimes Uncle Edgar would bring over their hogs for slaughter. It was Uncle Robert T's job to kill the hog. My brother Bubble was so amazed as he gave his accounts of Uncle Robert T shooting the hog right square between the eyes, and the pig falling to his knees, and Uncle Robert T's son James grabbing the hog's head and slitting his throat and the blood gushing from the hogs' neck. Pat and I wanted to know if the hog jumped around like the chickens. Bubble would give a demonstration of how the hog fell to his knees, groaned and quivered on the ground as the blood flowed from his body. Jimmy would chime in describing how it took three or four men to chain and hoist one hog up on the table. He said, "The hog slid down the sliding board, that was the biggest splash I ever saw! The boiling water filled the air with water and steam." He swore that the steam made snow that fell onto his jacket. "After a few minutes in the scalding water, the hog was hoisted to the table and the hairs were scraped from his hide, just like shaving" said Jimmy with so much excitement it was as if were seeing the event first hand. Bubble had to have his turn again, he said, "Once hairless, the hog was hung on the tripods upside down by his hind legs. With one smooth stroke of the knife the hog was split open and the hog's intestines and organs flowed out into the tin tub." Pat and I understood the reason Daddy wouldn't let us witness this event. We made frowning faces and said, "Gross, gross." I wished that we didn't have to clean the mess that flowed into the tin tub, but we did. Once the carcasses were hung, everyone would go home. The meat has to be good and cold to cut, that is why they had to wait until the thermometer dropped below freezing.

The next morning, Uncle Robert T and whomever else butchered a hog, would pick up their hog and take it home to cut and process. My uncles would take their portion of the innards from their hog home on Friday night. My aunts and cousins would be up early Saturday morning processing the innards since it was the women and children's job to clean and process the innards, as well as, cut and separate the smaller pieces of meat for sausage and lard. You need a large work area to process the hog meat.

The heart, kidneys, brains and sweetbreads are all eaten. The liver is cooked for liver pudding and the broth is mixed with meal to make "pawnhause." The bits of fat left from making the lard is used to make the world's best corn bread or cracklin' bread. The skin is fried for pork rinds. Absolutely no part of the hog is thrown away. Yes! The waste not, want not theory. Daddy said he had to eat so many "chittlins" (the intestines) when he was young, he gave the chittlins away, usually to someone who had no vested interest in butchering, but simply helped us with the butchering because it was the neighborly thing to do.

Since Daddy felt that it was not polite to give the chittlins away dirty, they had to be cleaned first. Cleaning chittlins was the worst job of all. The house smelled of hog meat for days. Most of the meat was stored in the meat house to be consumed throughout the year until the next butchering. The hog head was saved for the first meal of the new year. It was cooked with some mixed greens for good luck and prosperity.

Life was good. Daddy was living his dream. Early one Saturday morning in late August, Uncle Charles and Granddaddy John came to visit. Our first thought was that someone had died because we always went to Peola Mills to visit the Kilby side of the family, the Kilby's never visited us in Front Royal. Daddy was so overjoyed that he went out and slaughtered an extra couple of chickens for dinner and we had a big Sunday dinner and it wasn't even Sunday. They even bought some beer. Daddy didn't drink and it was the first time that we had beer in the house. Momma was pretty intrigued by the beer too. She got a bowl and a spoon, poured a taste in the bowl and we all tasted the beer. We decided that the beer looked and smelled like horse piss and it was nasty.

The good time turned sour when Granddaddy John told Daddy that old man Dick Finks wanted the 24 acres of land back. Daddy asked his father in an angry tone, "Is that the only reason you came to visit?" Granddaddy John responded, "Wilson, you know how the old man is, he's got it in his head that you didn't do anything with the land and now he wants it back. You are doing real good, you got a real nice place over here." Daddy shook his head in disbelief. He said, "I paid for that land with my soul and my dignity. Dick Finks is not my God. Just because he wants something, I am not going to bow down, kiss his ass and give it to him. I thought you came as a loving father to visit me and your grandchildren but you are just old man Dick Finks's Nigger coming to do his dirty work."

It wasn't a month later that Uncle Charles, Granddaddy John and old man Dick Finks showed up. Dad met them outside and he did not demonstrate his normal warm and friendly personality. They walked around to the side of the house. We all listened from the dining room window, Momma too. Dick Finks did most of the talking. He told Daddy that he wanted the deed to his land. Daddy told Dick Finks that he worked hard for that land and that he would not give it back. He told him to get off his property for disrespecting him. As Dick Finks left he said, "I will get my land back you uppity Nigger."

Chapter 2 _____

My Father Cried

My father cried because his father betrayed him, his children and his children's children for old man Dick Finks, the man he saw as his master and he did not have the power to stop him.

It was a weekday and Daddy didn't go to work as usual. Arvelon (Fee) and Roger came to visit. Momma and Daddy told us that they were going out and that we should be good children and mind Fee and Roger. I asked Fee if I could go for a walk and she said yes. I went to my secret hiding place down in the field among the snakes and wild life. There was a tree that God had made especially for me. The tree trunk grew straight up for about three feet, and then it bent over to make a perfect seat and continued its growth upward. I was fascinated with this tree. Every chance that I got, I would slip away from the house to sit in my tree, talk to God, think and write. As I sat in my tree, I heard something. I jumped from my perch and moved closer to the sounds. At first, I thought it was some kind of giant. Both arms were stretched toward the sky as if it were reaching for the clouds. It was screaming and crying, "Lord, Lord, Lord." As the creature came into focus it was Daddy. The words became clear, "Lord, I stretch my hands to Thee, no other help I know, If Thou withdraw Thyself from me, where shall I go?" Daddy fell to his knees. He cried like the deep, horrifying, uncontrollable, painful way people cry at funerals as he beat his head and fist on the ground. I cried too. I couldn't understand what was going on. I did not want Daddy to see me, so I crept through the bushes in the opposite direction and returned to the house.

By the time I got back to the house I was trembling. When Momma asked what was wrong, my brother answered, "stupid girl always hanging out down in the field, she probably saw a snake." I ran upstairs to my room and hid in my other secret hiding place. When the builders built the house, they did not nail one wall in the closet in my room. I would pull the piece of drywall open and hide behind the wall.

It was a year later that I found the transcript under the seat in Daddy's car. I kept reflecting back and thinking about the dates until I made the connection of what happened in the field that day that my Daddy cried. I also remembered that terrible whipping I got over at Aunt Mildred's when I was playing the game and sung about Daddy losing his land to old man Dick Finks. I read the transcript over and over again.

VIRGINIA: IN THE CIRCUIT COURT OF RAPPAHANNOCK COUNTY

- - - - - - - - - - - - - - - - - -

JOHN HENRY KILBY
            COMPLAINANT

   v.

JAMES WILSON KILBY AND
CATHERINE AUSBERRY KILBY
            DEFENDANTS

- - - - - - - - - - - - - - - - - -

           Rappahannock County Court House
           Washington, Virginia
           Wednesday, July 13, 1955

The above entitled matter came on for hearing at 10 o'clock a.m.,

BEFORE:

         HONORABLE RAYNER V. SNEAD, Judge

APPEARANCES:

JAMES W. FLETCHER, ESQ.   Sperryville, Virginia
                             Attorney for Complainant

JOSHUA L. ROBINSON, ESQ.   Luray, Virginia
RICHARD N. BROOKE, ESQ.   Front Royal, Virginia
                             Attorneys for Defendants

PROCEEDINGS

(Opening statements were made by Counsel for both sides)

P.M. FINKS

was called as a witness for the Complainant, and being first duly sworn, was examined and testified as follows:

DIRECT EXAMINATION

BY MR. FLETCHER:

Q Please state your name and age.

A P.M. Finks. I am 66 years old and will be 67 on the 7th of October.

Q Do you know the Complainant John Henry Kilby?

A Yes

Q Do you know the Defendant?

A Yes

Q Mr. Finks, how long has John Kilby worked for you and your sister?

A Fifty years or more.

Q Which of his sons were born on the farm?

A All of them.

Q In 1938, How many of the were working for you?

A Well, he was, and Charles and Willie I am sure.

Q In 1936 did you learn that a track of 24 acres was for sale?

A Yes.

Q Did you have any conversation regarding that fact with John Kilby?

A Yes.

Q As a result, did you or John Kilby attempt to buy the property?

A Yes.

Q Was there any discussion of Wilson Kilby at that time?

A Not a word!

Q   Was there any agreement with Wilson Kilby that if he stayed on and worked for you that you would. . .

MR. ROBINSON: I object: He is leading the witness.

MR. FLETCHER CONTINUED DIRECT EXAMINATION

Q   Did you have any agreement?

A   He never worked for me.

Q   Did Wilson Kilby come to you with the thought that he would buy this property?

A   No.

Q   Was there any negotiation on behalf of John Kilby for the purchase of this land?

MR. ROBINSON: I object to the form of the questioning and the alternative:

Q   Did you attempt to buy this land from Effie Diedrich?

A   Yes.

Q   For yourself?

MR. ROBINSON: I object:

JUDGE SNEAD: I think perhaps you are leading the witness. We all know what the pleadings have been. Let him explain in his own words.

MR. FLETCHER CONTINUED DIRECT EXAMINATION

Q   What were your negotiations with Mrs. Diedrich?

A   She came up to my house and wanted to sell this property. He went on and paid me $400.00 and said he would pay me back as long as he worked. I thought my sister would think hard of me if I took him away from her.

MR. ROBINSON: I object: The witness is not responsive.

JUDGE SNEAD: Just tell what you know about it.

MR. FINKS: I didn't even know under whose name the deed was made.

MR. ROBINSON: I object to that.

JUDGE SNEAD TO THE JURY: This witness' opinions are not admissable.

MR. FLETCHER CONTINUES DIRECT EXAMINATION

Q   Do you know where John Kilby got $400.00?

A   No, sir.

Q· Do you know whether he had it in the bank or on his person?

A   I just know he paid me $400.00 down on it.

Q   This $1200, where did you get it?

A   I got it out of the bank, and I paid Mrs. Diedrich.

Q   Did Wilson Kilby obligate himself to pay you back any portion of the $1200?

A   No, sir.

MR. ROBINSON: I move to strike that question.

JUDGE SNEAD: granted.

MR. FLETCHER CONTINUES DIRECT EXAMINATION

Q   Who paid the taxes on the land?

A   I did.

Q   What happened to the deed after Mr. Strother drew it?

A   I gave it to the old man and he put it in the trunk.

Q   You don't know that he put it in the trunk do you?

A   No

Q   Did you ever have any conversation with Wilson Kilby?

A   No sir.

Q   In the summer of 1954, did you and Uncle John Kilby have any discussion about this land?

A   No.

Q   Have you ever been to see Wilson Kilby concerning the land?

A   Yes.

Q   Who was with you?

A   The old man and Charles. We tried to make an agreement with him, but he wouldn't even talk to us.

Q When was the first time you knew Wilson laid claim to this land?

A Last year.

Q Until that time did you ever know he laid claim to the land?

A No sir.

Q Who did lay claim to it?

A The old man.

Q Has anyone paid you back the $1200?

A No

Q Did you make a gift of that $1200?

A No.

Q What is the status of the $ 1200 at this time?

A I don't know what you mean.

Q How do you regard the $1200? Have you written it off your books?

A No. He still owes it to me.

Q When did you and your sister divide up on the home place?

A Before 1938 I reckon.

Q Were you operating as a partnership?

A Yes.

Q Did you operate in business with her or separate?

A We were separate.

Q At the time this deed was made were you separate?

A Yes.

Q Has any work been done on this 24 acres of land?

A Yes, $200 on the house, new windows and floors, we done some ditching and put in a line fence.

Q At the request of John Kilby or Wilson Kilby?

MR. ROBINSON: I object:

JUDGE SNEAD: Objection sustained.

MR. FLETCHER CONTINUES DIRECT EXAMINATION

Q Did anyone request that you do it?

A No.

Q Have you and John Kilby made any settlement on it?

A No.

Q Have you ever had any accounting?

A No.

Q Where does your sister live now?

A She lives with me. She's been with me about four years-since she sold her place.

Q Was Charles Kilby with you and Uncle John when the deed was drawn?

A No. Mr. Strother drew the deed.

Q Who instructed Mr. Strother and Mrs. Diedrich whose name the deed should be placed in? What name did you tell him to place it in?

A He placed it in this boys' name. I thought my sister would get mad if I took this man away from her, so I went on and had it put in the boy's name.

Q Did Wilson ever work for you?

A No, never.

Q Did you have any reason to make a loan to Wilson Kilby?

A No.

Q That is all.

CROSS EXAMINATION

BY MR. ROBINSON:

Q Who was Wilson Kilby working for in 1936?

A For my sister.

Q Who was he working for in 1935?

A Same place.

Q   How long did he work there?

A   He was born there.

Q   What year did you and your sister split up?

A   I am not sure.

Q   You don't know when you split up?

A   No, sir.

Q   Was he working for you in 1935?

A   No. He never has worked for me. I never paid him wages.

Q   How about John Henry Kilby?

A   He worked for my sister and myself until we split up.

Q   Was John Henry Kilby working for you when this deed was drawn?

A   That is none of your business!

JUDGE SNEAD: You will have to answer the question. Go ahead, sir.

MR. FINKS: He was working for my sister.

MR. ROBINSON CONTINUES CROSS EXAMINATION

Q   Is your sister here in the county today?

A   Yes.

Q   I'm not sure whether or not it will be necessary to call your sister.

MR. ROBINSON TO JUDGE SNEAD: Will you please direct the sheriff to issue a subpoena for her. (This was done)

MR. ROBINSON CONTINUES CROSS EXAMINATION

Q   When did John Kilby last work for you?

A   I don't know.

Q   Was it before or after this property was bought?

A   I don't know.

Q   How long before you bought the 24 acres did you split up?

A   I don't know.

Q   Was it two weeks or 10 years?

A   I don't know. I don't know exactly.

Q You and your sister split up between 1936 and 1938 didn't you?

A I don't know.

Q You remember what happened when the deed was signed don't you?

A I don't remember exactly what.

Q Your memory seems pretty good to me.

A I don't know just when we separated.

Q What year did you get back together?

A Four years ago.

Q Was John Kilby working for you then?

A He was working for her and is working for her now.

Q What did John Henry Kilby have to do with you?

A I didn't have anything to do with him.

Q You are sure of that?

A I can't remember.

Q Are you sure that John Henry Kilby wasn't working for you on the 28th day of November, 1936, when this deed was signed?

A I don't remember. He hasn't worked for me since we separated.

Q I don't mean to draw this out but I am trying to get the facts. You don't remember whether John Henry Kilby was working for you or your sister?

A He was working for her, but I don't remember whether we were partners or not.

MR. FLETCHER: If Mr. Robinson is really interested, he can get the report.

MR. ROBINSON CONTINUES CROSS EXAMINATION

Q John Henry Kilby was working for you wasn't he?

A I can't tell you, I just don't remember.

JUDGE SNEAD: That is enough of that line of questioning.

MR. ROBINSON CONTINUES CROSS EXAMINATION

Q   James Wilson Kilby was working for you in 1936 wasn't he?

A   He never worked for me. I told you that about six times!!!!!!

Q   You and your sister were partners?

A   He might have worked for her, but not for me.

Q   Didn't you just tell us that you and your sister were partners?

A   I told you all I know.

Q   You and your sisters were you not?

JUDGE SNEAD: Mr. Finks has answered that question.

MR. ROBINSON CONTINUES CROSS EXAMINATION

Q   I hope I can clear this up. Is it correct Mr. Finks, that on the 18th day of November, you don't remember whether or not you and your sister were partners?

JUDGE SNEAD: Don't answer that.

MR.. ROBINSON: May it please the court. Mr. Fletcher says he can get the answers. Can we recess until we find the answers?

> (Whereupon court was recessed while answers were found.)

> (Court reconvened at 11 o'clock a.m. After 15 minutes recess period.)

MR. ROBINSON: Mr. Finks, I hope you don't think I have been trying to brow-beat you. I have been merely trying to get answers.

Q   Have you now refreshed your memory Mr. Finks, by looking at the Clerk's records?

A   Yes

Q   After this split-up, did John Henry Kilby work for you?

A   I moved over to my place and never had anything to do with John Henry Kilby.

Q   Who pays him?

A   I rent my farm to my sister and she pays him.

Q Do you have any idea how much she pays him?

A No, sir.

Q Do you mean to say that you paid out $1200 for him and you don't know what he is making? When was he supposed to pay you back?

A Whenever he got it. He was with my sister all his life.

Q Did you have any interest in the welfare of John Henry Kilby in 1936?

A I never did.

Q You never cared about Him?

A I never said I didn't care about him.

Q Who bought this property from Effie Diedrich?

A I did.

Q How did you pay for it?

A I gave her a check for it.

Q Whose money was it?

A I paid her with my money, whose money do you suppose?

Q Do you have a canceled check?

A She got the money and that is all she cared about.

Q Was it your money?

A Certainly it was my money.

Q I understand you were not giving any money to anybody.

A No, I wasn't.

Q Was John Kilby working for you then?

A He was working on the home place for 50 or 60 years.

Q If Mr. Finks would just answer the question we could get on with this.

A He keeps asking the same question all the time.

MR. FLETCHER: You have to understand the witness' temperament.

JUDGE SNEAD TO MR. FINKS: I don't mean to be impolite, but please be quiet!

MR. ROBINSON CONTINUES CROSS EXAMINATION

Q   Mr. Finks, who made the agreement to buy the property from Mrs. Jenkins and Mrs. Diedrich?

A   I did.

Q   Did Mrs. Jenkins have anything to do with it?

A   She was in on it, but she died soon after.

Q   Did you ever talk to her?

A   It belonged to old Mrs. Jenkins and she came up by my place and asked me if I wanted to buy it. I said yes.

Q   Who did you buy the property from?

A   From both Mrs. Diedrich and Mrs. Jenkins.

Q   Who did you pay?

A   I paid Mrs. Diedrich.

Q   Who did you make the check out to?

A   Mrs. Diedrich.

Q   In Mr. Strother's office?

A   Yes.

Q   Who were present in Mr. Strother's office?

A   Mr. Jenkins, Mrs. Diedrich, I don't know where Mr. Diedrich was.

Q   John Henry Kilby wasn't there was he?

A   No.

Q   He paid some on the property didn't he?

A   He paid $400.00.

Q   Who did he pay it to?

A   To me.

Q   When did he pay you?

A   After I paid Mrs. Diedrich the full price. He said he would pay me back as long as he worked for me. I said O.K. As long as you work for my sister and my mother, go ahead.

Q   Who did Mrs. Diedrich sell it to?

A   To Molly Jenkins.

Q   Who did Jenkins sell it to?

A   I couldn't tell you.

Q   Who did you buy it from?

A   I brought it from Jenkins and Mrs. Diedrich. Both of them came here, and I bought it and paid the $1600 acting for myself.

Q   This deed, Mr. Finks, who did you get it from?

A   Mr. Strother gave it to me.

Q   You took it and had it recorded?

A   Yes.

Q   Do you remember how many papers were mailed to you?

A   I don't know.

Q   Well, who did you give the papers to?

A   The old man. I gave him one paper.

Q   One paper was all you gave him?

A   That was all.

Q   Did you know that when this property was bought James Wilson Kilby was only 17 years old?

A   I didn't care what his age was.

Q   You didn't ask John Henry Kilby to sign a note?

A   No. He lived there all his life and I said just pay me back when you get the money. I'm not trying to tell you any lie.

Q   How long have you used the property?

A   Ever since I bought it.

Q   Who paid the taxes?

A   I paid the taxes, and he said go ahead and use it.

Q   Did you pay any rent?

A   No. I kept everything up. I did all that has been done on it.
    I never paid any rent.

Q   Did you get all of the crops?

A   Not all.

Q   What return has John Henry Kilby gotten from it?

A   He lives with us and gets his living on it.

Q   Have you ever lived on it?

A   I ain't never lived on it.

Q   Where is he living now?

A   With my sister. He lives with all of us.

Q   With you or with your sister?

A   With all of us.

Q   What return has he gotten from it since it has been deeded to his son?

A   I don't know. He never got much I tell you.

Q   You rented it out on shares?

A   Yes.

Q   When a tenant finished taking in his crop, who did he pay?

A   Nobody. He got so much of the profit, and I got some of it. I got as much as anybody else. The owner got half the crop.

Q   Who did he give the other half to?

A   To me.

Q   Did he turn it over to you?

A   Yes.

Q   Not to your sister?

A   To me. I don't want to be confused by you.

MR. FLETCHER: They all got it and it went into a common till.

MR. ROBINSON CONTINUES CROSS EXAMINATION

Q   Did you ever take the deed to James Wilson Kilby and ask him to sign it?

A   Yes.

Q　Who did you ask him to give the paper to?

A　The old man.

Q　Do you have any interest in how this case comes out?

A　Do I care? Sure I do. Wilson never did anything for me. I want to do something for someone who has done something for me.

Q　If the jury should decide that John Henry Kilby is entitled to the property, do you expect the old man to give you anything from it?

A　I expect him to give me what I have in it.

MR. FLETCHER: I object! That is immaterial.

JUDGE SNEAD: Mr. Finks, what questions are you answering now? Please answer what you are asked, that is all we ask you to do.

MR. FINKS: I do the best I know how.

MR. ROBINSON CONTINUES CROSS EXAMINATION

Q　Are you expecting John Henry Kilby to deed this property to you?

A　I don't know whether he will or not.

Q　Do you expect him to?

A　No, sir. It's his.

Q　Is it correct that you that you expect him to deed you this property, or pay you the $1200?

A　If he happens to pay the $1200 I don't know.

JUDGE SNEAD: That is not the answer to the question.

MR. ROBINSON CONTINUES CROSS EXAMINATION

Q　Have you ever at any time since the 28th of November, 1936, asked John Henry Kilby to pay you back any part of the $1200.

A　I never had, before or after either. Whenever he got the money he could pay me.

Q　Have you ever pushed him?

A　No.

Q Have you ever asked James Wilson Kilby for the $1200?

A I never asked him for anything.

Q Have you ever told anyone that the property belonged to James Wilson Kilby?

Q No.

Q Where was he living when he got married?

A I don't know.

Q Do you remember when he planned to leave?

A No. I never tried to keep him.

Q Did you ever have a conversation with his wife?

A No.

Q Do you know Ashley Carpenter?

A I don't think enough of him to ask him anything.

MR. ROBINSON: I object: He should not give reasons.

JUDGE SNEAD: Gentlemen of the jury, the opinions of Mr. Finks have no bearing on the case.

MR. FINKS CONTINUED

A I never had any words with Carpenter.

MR. FLETCHER: Mr. Finks, just answer the judge or Mr. Robinson's questions, then stop immediately.

MR. ROBINSON CONTINUES CROSS EXAMINATION

Q Mr. Finks, do you remember when Ashley Carpenter once tried to rent the property from you?

A Yes.

Q Do you remember who you told him the property belonged to?

A No. I never told him anything.

Q No further questions.

MR. FLETCHER:

Q   When you paid this consideration to Mrs. Diedrich, did you pay it on your behalf or for Wilson Kilby?

A   For myself.

Q   Do you recall whether John Kilby gave you $400 before or after you went to Mr. Strother's office?

A   After.

Q   Is there any difference in the quality of the 24 acres since you bought it?

MR. ROBINSON: I object:

JUDGE SNEAD: Objection over-rule.

MR. ROBINSON: Exception.

MR. FLETCHER CONTINUED

Q   My question was "Is there any difference in the quality of the 24 acres since you bought it?"

A   I have limed it and nourished it.

Q   Was there any brush on it in 1936, or did it grow from 1936 on up?

A   You never saw such a place in your life. It was just a lot of brush land.

Q   Mr. Robinson asked you questions about whether or not you paid any rent to John Kilby for the place. Who paid for cleaning up the property?

A   I did.

Q   Who paid for the mature?

A   I did.

Q   Who paid for the ditching?

A   I did. I paid $200 and some cents for house repairs. I put in a half mile of barbed wire. I paid the taxes. I paid the insurance.

Q   Where did John Kilby's children eat?

A   Right at our house.

Q   Has John Kilby paid any interest on the money?

A   No.

Q   How much money do you figure he owes you at the moment?

A $1200 on the place, so I figure he owes me $1200.

Q   Have you ever asked John Kilby for interest on your money?

A   No, sir.

No further questions.

> (At this point the sheriff reported that Miss Edith Finks
> was sick and would not be able to attend court.)

CHARLES KILBY

Was called as a witness, and being first duly sworn, was examined and testified as follows:

DIRECT EXAMINATION

BY MR. ROBINSON:

Q   Your name is Charles Kilby?

A   Yes.

Q   Where do you live?

A   With Miss Edith.

Q   How old are you?

A   I will be 41 on the 8th of October.

Q   Can you give us the names and ages of the other children?

A   I am the oldest. Willie is about a year younger. Wilson is about five years younger- about 36. Mildred is about 35, and Irene is 23 or 24. I think John is 24, and Polly would be 33. They all grew up at Miss Edith Finks.

Q   Where were you working in 1936?

A   At Miss Edith Finks.

Q   And Willie?

A   There too.

Q   When did Mr. Dick and Miss Edith split up?

A   About 25 or 26 years ago.

Q   Do you know when this land was bought?

A   About 1937.

Q   Were any of you working for Dick Finks at that time?

A   No.

Q   Do you know anything about the actual deed?

A   Nothing. Wilson told me that Mr. Dick bought it for daddy, and that the property was in his name.

Q   Did he explain why Mr. Dick didn't want Miss Edith to find out, that she might think they were all going away?

A   He knew it was daddy's all along.

Q   When did you hear that the property was Wilson's?

A   Not until I heard Wilson say it was his.

Q   When was that?

A   Last August.

Q   When did he say it was in his name?

MR. FLETCHER: I object to that:

MR. ROBINSON CONTINUES DIRECT EXAMINATION

Q   How long after 1936 did Wilson know it was in his name but being held for his father?

A   It was about two or three years after it was bought. It was in pretty bad shape. Some was cleared, but not much. It's in good condition now.

Q   What was done?

A   It was ditched and cleaned up.

Q   Is Mr. Finks doing the farming now?

A   Miss Edith is.

Q   Who feeds the stock?

A   Mr. Dick, Mr. Dick has the cattle.

Q   Does Miss Edith feed any of it?

A   I don't know.

Q   Has your father gotten anything out of this place?

A   I don't know.

Q   What claim has Wilson made to it?

A   I don't Know.

Q   What do you know about last August?

A   He claimed he owned it and brought suit.

Q   Who brought suit?

A   Daddy.

Q   What kind of work did you do?

A   House carpenter. I worked for Mr. Dick, and we changed work back and forth with Miss Edith and Mr. Dick. We always worked both farms together.

Q   Did Wilson work on both farms too?

A   No. I did, and my father did.

Q   What kind of work did Wilson do?

A   He worked on the farm. We all went back and forth to thresh wheat.

Q   How much was he paid?

A   I don't know.

Q   How much were you paid?

A   I don't know.

Q   When did you start getting a regular salary?

A   When I was old enough to work-about 21 years old.

Q   You are 41 now, so you must have been 21 in 1935. You didn't do any work until you were 21 did you?

A   Yes, sir.

Q   How old were you?

A   When I was 10 or 11 I was feeding the chickens. I plowed and mowed the lawn.

Q   Did you do anything else?

A   I don't know.

Q　What did Wilson do?

A　I don't know.

Q　You lived in the same house didn't you?

A　I don't know what he was doing.

Q　Did he do any work around Miss Edith's House?

A　He fed the chickens.

Q　How old was he?

A　About the same age as me.

Q　How old was that?

A　About 10 years old.

Q　When did you start to do man's work?

A　When I was about 18 years old.

Q　You stated you were 21 when you received a salary. How much were you paid?

A　I got $250 a year.

Q　How long did you get that?

A　About five years.

Q　When was the last day you worked?

A　In January, 1954.

Q　You haven't done any work since then?

A　Nothing much.

Q　What were you paid in 1953?

MR. FLETCHER: That is immaterial:

MR. ROBINSON CONTINUES DIRECT EXAMINATION

Q　What were you paid when you were 18 years old?

A　I don't know.

Q　When you were 19?

A　I don't know.

Q　When you were 20?

A　I don't know.

Q   What about 21?

A   I don't know.

Q   What was James Wilson Kilby paid during the year he was 18?

A   I don't know.

Q   Would your answer be the same to all the questions?

A   I don't know.

No further questions.

MR. FLETCHER: You used the words "changed work"- how high did you go in school?

A   Fourth grade.

Q   What did you mean by it?

Q   You said you would help thresh wheat.

A   She would help us with a crew and we would help him.

Q   So you don't mean that you went over and worked as his employee?

A   No.

MR. ROBINSON: I object:

MR. FLETCHER: Do you know what the word exchange means?

A   No. He would pay her back by sending his men over to help her.

That is all.

CONNER JENKINS

Was called as a witness, and being first duly sworn, was examined and testified as follows:

DIRECT EXAMINATION

BY MR. FLETCHER:

Q   What is your name and age?

A   Conner Jenkins, I am 51 years old.

Q   Are you a farmer?

A   Yes.

Q Have you ever share-cropped the 24 acres which adjoins the land of Mr. Finks and the Hershberger property?

A Yes.

Q Do you know who owns it.

MR. ROBINSON: I object: That calls for a conclusion.

MR. FLETCHER: You have worked on it?

A I done plenty of work on it. I cleared the land off.

Q Did you at any time have occasion to buy this land?

A Yes. I said something to Wilson, and he said it belonged to Uncle John and Mr. Finks.

Q Where and when did you approach him with a view to buying it?

A It was a long time ago. I told him someone told me the land belonged to him. He said, "What piece of land?" He told me it didn't belong to him, it belonged to his daddy.

That is all.

BY MR. ROBINSON:

Q Who did you make the arrangements with for working on this property?

A Uncle John.

Q When you were interested in buying this property, how did you find out it belonged to Wilson?

A A number of people told me.

Q Was Mr. Finks one of them?

A No, Uncle John said it belonged to him. Mr. Dodson said something about it.

Q When you cut crops, did you work for anyone?

A I just share-cropped.

Q Who was there?

A Uncle John and Charles.

Q   Was Mr. Finks there?

A   Sometimes.

Q   Who took charge of the conversation when Mr. Finks was there?

A   Uncle John did.

That is all.

MR. FLETCHER: How many years did you share-crop this property?

A   10 years

Q   Did you ever see Wilson Kilby during that time?

A   No, not a word in the world.

Thank you very much. No further questions.

> (Whereupon, at 12:30 o'clock p.m., a luncheon recess was taken, to reconvene at 1:30 o'clock, p.m.)

JOHN HENRY KILBY

Was called as a witness, and being first duly sworn, was examined and testified as follows:

DIRECT EXAMINATION

BY MR. FLETCHER

Q   State your full name and age please.

A   John Henry Kilby. I am 73 years old.

Q   What school did you attend?

A   A little one-room school down on the John Hawkins place.

Q   Can you read and write?

A   Read a little, but not write.

Q   Are you the father of these boys?

A   Yes.

Q   How long have you lived with the Finks?

A   About 50 Or 60 years. I started to work when I was 17 years old.

Q   Do you recall when Mr. Dick and Miss Edith divided up operation of the farm?

A   About 30 years ago.

Q   Now, did you buy any land after Mr. Dick and Miss Edith split up their property?

A   I bought this land after they split up- about 10 years I guess.

Q   How much did you pay for the property?

A $1600.

Q   Did you pay any of the money yourself?

A   I paid $400.

Q   Where did you get it?

A   From labor. I had it in the bank.

Q   What bank?

A   The Culpepper National Bank.

Q   Did Wilson give you any of the money?

A   No.

Q   Where did you get the balance of the money?

A   Mr. Dick paid for the place and I was supposed to pay him,

Q   How much did you borrow?

MR. ROBINSON: I object: He is leading the witness.

JUDGE SNEAD: Objection over-ruled.

MR. ROBINSON: Exception.

MR. FLETCHER CONTINUES DIRECT EXAMINATION

Q   How much did you borrow from Mr. Finks?

A   The rest outside of the $400.

Q   Who was Wilson working for at that time?

A   Miss Edith. We all stayed together.

Q Did he work for Mr. Dick?

A He didn't do as much.

Q With respect to you, Has Wilson done more for you than your other children?

A No.

Q Do you have any reason to prefer any child that you have?

A No.

Q Have you ever preferred Wilson over any of the other children?

A No.

Q Did you ever make him a gift?

A No.

Q How did the title come to be in his name?

A Because Mr. Dick didn't want to have any trouble between him and Miss Edith.

Q Didn't any discussion take place with respect to whose name the property should be put in?

A Mr. Dick didn't want Miss Edith to think he was trying to take us away from her.

Q What reason did you have for putting Wilson's name on it?

A It was just to put down a disturbance. I thought he was honest.

Q The property was put in Wilson's name?

A Yes.

Q Has Mr. Dick asked you to deed the property to him?

A He said I could pay him the money, or deed the property.

Q Has he demanded that you pay him?

A No.

Q Have you had any conversation with Wilson.

A No.

Q Before last year had you discussed the property?

A He said he could get the money and pay for it, and I could pay Mr. Dick.

Q When did he come to you with that statement?

A About 10 years ago.

Q What did you tell him?

A I said as long as Mr. Dick was doing like he was, I would let it go along as it was.

Q Did Wilson claim it was his property at that time?

A Not to me.

Q How did he come to you?

A Just talking- like anyone would.

Q Did he tell you he could get the money?

A Yes.

Q Has he ever laid claim that this land was his own?

A No. Last fall when this letter was wrote about plowing alfalfa and that it was going to be sold in so many days-there was no name signed to the letter.

MR. ROBINSON: This letter was not brought out before.

MR. FLETCHER: Did you then go to see Wilson about the land?

A I told him to get it straightened out, and I couldn't pay for it to let it go back to Mr. Dick. He said he would, but he hasn't yet.

Q What did you do after he refused to straighten it up?

A I came to you.

Q Did you sign any papers about this property? Did you bring this suit?

A I guess so.

Q May I ask if this is your signature? (Whereupon he offered some papers for Mr. Kilby's inspection.)

A Yes.

Q   Did Wilson pay any part of the money paid to Mr. Dick?

A   No

Q   Did you intend to make a gift of that property to Wilson?

A   No.

Q   Did you intend that it should be an advancement of his share of your estate in the event of your death?

A   No.

That is all.

CROSS EXAMINATION

BY MR. ROBINSON:

Q   How old was Wilson when this property was bought?

A   17 years old.

Q   Who was he working for?

A   Miss Edith.

Q   Was she the only one he ever worked for?

A   Yes.

Q   What kind of work did he do for her?

A   He fed the chickens and turkeys, and did a little work in the field.

Q   How much was he getting paid?

A   I don't know. She hired him and paid him.

Q   You wanted to see that he was being paid the proper amount didn't you?

A   He didn't tell me what he was paid.

Q   Was he satisfied?

A   I guess so.

Q   Did he ever say anything about leaving?

A   I never objected to his going.

Q   When did he first say he was going?

A   After he was married.

Q   Did he ever tell you he was leaving?

A   He never said he was dissatisfied.

Q   What kind of a dispute was there between Mr. Finks and his sister?

A   They both thought they could do better by themselves. They just had a friendly separation of their business interests. No one was mad as far as I know.

Q   At the time the property was bought, Wilson was working for Miss Edith and so were you. Did Edith ever ask you where Wilson got the money to buy the property?

A   No. it didn't make any difference to her whose name it was in.

Q   She wouldn't have known if the property was in your name would she?

A   No.

Q   She didn't know anything about it until last year, did she?

A   No.

Q   It wouldn't have made a difference whose name the property was in would it?

A   I don't think so.

Q   Who did you buy the property from?

A   Mr. Dick Finks.

Q   Who did he buy it from?

A   From Miss Jenkins and Mrs. Diedich.

Q   You didn't buy it from them did you?

A   No.

Q   When Mr. Finks bought it you were not in the picture were you?

A   He bought it on his own.

Q   Did you buy it with the $400 from the Finks?

A   When he bought it, he bought it for himself. He let me have it after he bought it.

Q   Was that when you paid the $400?

A   Yes.

Q   When were you supposed to pay him back?

A   No particular time.

Q   He never charged you any interest?

A   He said as long as I was tending the land it would be O.K.

Q   There was no special time when this money was to be paid back?

A   No.

Q   You said you were working for Edith at this time. How much were you making?

A   I don't know. I was making and spending.

Q   You got a salary didn't you?

A   I worked by the year.

Q   How much did you get by the year?

A $800 or $900.

Q   Were you paid in cash?

A   I don't know. I was paid at Christmas.

Q   How much did you get in cash?

A   Whatever was coming to me. Sometimes I drew some of it in the year– when I needed it.

Q   Did that include your food, your place of living, and your clothes? You had to buy clothes didn't you?

A   She bought them in addition to the $800.

Q   When did the boys start to get paid?

A   I don't remember. Whenever she needed them, she paid them.

Q   Did Wilson get paid every week?

A   I don't know. I didn't pay any attention.

Q   Do you remember when he got married?

A   Yes.

Q   How long did he live with you after he got married?

A   In April and he left Christmas.

Q   Did you ever suggest that he and his wife live on this property?

A   No.

Q   Did Mr. Finks ever suggest any such thing?

A   No.

Q   Did you ever suggest that he go to the Eastland Place and get higher wages?

A   I never suggested it - I had no right to.

Q   You mean they could have lived there if they wanted to?

A   I reckon.

Q   I just have a few more questions. How much have you made off this property?

A   I haven't made anything.

Q   Who made it?

A   Mr. Finks has been tending it.

Q   Has Mr. Finks asked Wilson to pay the $1200?

A   No.

Q   Have you discussed this case with Mr. Finks?

A   No.

Q   Have you talked to Mr. Finks about it?

A   I don't know what you mean.

Q   Before you bought suit you talked to Mr. Finks didn't you?

A   I had no right to talk to him.

Q   When you went to see the lawyer you went with Mr. Finks didn't you?

A   Yes.

Q   Have you and Mr. Finks ever discussed what ought to be done with it?

A   He knows what ought to be done with it.

Q   What does he want you to do with it if you get it?

A   If I get it, I will get a living in my old days.

Q   Has he ever told you he wants you to deed it over to him?

A   No.

Q   Did he tell you to pay the $1200?

A   No.

Q   Do you think Mr. Finks would let you keep the property and pay the $1200 too?

A   My wife got sick, but I intend to pay the rest on it.

Q   Has he ever asked you to have a deed made out for this property?

A   No.

Q   Didn't he say that he would pay the $400 back if he got the property?

A   No. He expects me to pay him and I will own the property.

MR. FLETCHER: Uncle John, when you went to see Wilson Kilby with Mr. Finks, who did you ask him to make the deed to?

A   Wilson was supposed to sign it, but he wouldn't.

Q   Mr. Robinson asked some questions about when this property was bought. When you had this conversation with Mr. Finks, was that before or after the deed was made for Wilson? How long after that was the deed made?

A   Five or six days.

Q   When that was done did he discuss whose name was to be put in?

A   He said in Wilson's name, to put down a disturbance.

MR. ROBINSON: Had Mr. Finks already paid for the property when you agreed to buy it from him?

A   Yes.

Q   When you asked your son to sign this deed, whose name was on the deed? Was it to you, or to Mr. Finks?

A   Mr. Finks was supposed to see that the land was fixed up.

Q   Was it made so that you could get the land, or that Mr. Finks could get the land?

A   I don't remember.

MR. FLETCHER: I asked you whether you agreed to take the property and Mr. Finks agreed to get it for you. You said five or six days passed before the deed was made. Now, did you know of your own knowledge, when the money was turned over to Mrs. Diedrich.

A   I wasn't present.

(Whereupon the court and counsel retired to chambers,
where the following proceedings were had):

MR. ROBINSON: May it please the court, we move to strike the
evidence of the complainant on the grounds that there was no proof of
express trust. Edwards against Edwards 139, Williams against Powers
139. When the consideration is paid by the father for the son, the
presumption is that it is a gift. (2) That the evidence does not show
that the complainant paid all of the consideration. At the time the consideration was paid, the money belonged to Finks. Whether there was a
subsequent transaction between Finks and the Complainant is immaterial.
It must arise at the time of the complaint and not subsequent thereto.
Jurisprudence, Section 28. (3) That the evidence of the complainant
does not meet the high standards necessary to meet high trust. It is
not clear and explicit enough to prove any kind of trust. Finks gave
some evidence of hiding the transaction from his sister, The witness
and Finks were bit on bad terms and he knew of no unfortunate
consequences if the sister knew of the transaction. If any ill feeling
would be caused by taking of the property in John Henry Kilby's name,
the same ill feeling would result because James Wilson Kilby took the
property in his name. The evidence of the complainant, on the whole,
falls short of being cognizant. I move to strike the evidence."

MR. FLETCHER; My resistance to the motion, Your Honor, is that you
have previously ruled that an expressed trust is not necessary and it
can arise where the evidence is clear. Now, in this case, the failure to
prove the second point mentioned. The consideration was paid in the
office of Mr. Strother. Kilby obligated himself to pay the consideration.
It was made to keep down any ill feeling between Finks and his sister,
therefore, whether the consideration is paid directly by Kilby or his
agent is immaterial. Kilby stated he was obligated. Finks stated that
possibly there had been a failure to establish a trust prior to the time
that the actual deed was made, and he elected to have Kilby have his
rights and they decided to take it in Kilby's name. It was agreed to
have it in the name of John Henry Kilby to be held in the name of
James Wilson Kilby, to prevent Miss Edith from thinking that Mr. Dick
was trying to take away her employees. Kilby has stated that he took
the property away from Mr. Dick after he (Mr. Dick) bought it.

He used the term "bought" necessarily meaning to "negotiate" for it. I further state that as to the payment, he personally stated that he didn't know when the money passed between Mr. Finks and Mrs. Diedrich. He thought it was being passed....

MR. ROBINSON: I object:

JUDGE SNEAD: Objection over-ruled.

MR. ROBINSON; Exception.

JAMES WILSON KILBY

Was called as a witness, and being first duly sworn, was examined and testified as follows:

DIRECT EXAMINATION

BY MR. ROBINSON

Q   Tell the jury your name.

A   James Wilson Kilby

Q   How old are you?

A   I am 37 years old.

Q   You are the son of John Henry Kilby?

A   Yes.

Q   Where were you born?

A   In Rappahannock County.

Q   Who did you live with?

A   Emma, Edith and P.M.

Q   Where was your father working?

A   He was working for the three of them.

Q   Did you ever work for these people?

A   Yes, all of them.

Q   How old were you?

A   Just a kid- about 10 years old.

Q   What did you do when you first started to work?

A   Everything. I shined the floors and waited table.

Q   Where did you live?

A   My mother and father worked for them and we lived in the kitchen side of the house.

Q   Whose property was it?

A   It belonged to all three of them.

Q   At the time you got to be 17 years old, who were you working for?

A   Emma, Edith, and Dick.

Q   What kind of work were you doing?

A   Anything that the men were doing except drive the team.

Q   Were you paid?

A   No.

Q   When the children were growing up what did you do?

A   We all worked there but Charles. He was the exception. The rest were not raised like Charles. He had more freedom.

Q   As you got older what did you do?

A   I worked for the three of them.

Q   By the time you were 17 were you still working for them?

A   Yes.

Q   Did you know about any separation between Dick and Miss Edith?

A   Not definitely.

Q   Who did you consider you were working for?

A   The three of them. They all owned the property.

Q   When was the first time you found out about this property?

A   In 1935.

Q   How did you find out?

A   Mr. Finks told me he would buy the property for me.

Q   For whom?

A   For me.

Q   What did you do after that?

A   I stayed on.

Q   How much were you paid at that time?

A   Just anything the Finks' gave me. Sometimes $5.00 or $10.00. Just a little bit- a little money at Christmas time.

Q   How much did any of the Finks pay you in cash up until the time you were 21 years old over a period of a year?

A   It didn't amount to $50.00.

Q   Did you discuss with your father or Mr. Finks what your plans for the future were?

A   Yes.

Q   Did you ever tell your father or Mr. Finks that you planned to leave?

A   Yes. I told them I planned to go to New York because I was dissatisfied working for nothing. Mr. Finks told me if I stayed on and worked for Edith and his mother he would give me the $1200, so I stayed.

Q   Were you present when the deed was drawn?

A   No.

Q   Who did he tell you the property belonged to?

A   Me.

Q   Did you owe Mr. Finks any money?

A   No. I was suppose to stay and work for Edith and Emma.

Q   Who asked you to stay there?

A   Mr. Finks.

Q   Did he say how much was to be paid?

A   No.

Q   After this property was conveyed in your name, how long did you stay on this property?

A   Until the year I was 25.

Q   What year was that?

A   I left in 1943, so that would be about seven years.

Q   This property was conveyed in 1936. Did they pay you any salary in 1936?

A   No.

Q   In 1937?

A   No.

Q   What kind of work were you doing?

A   Anything a man was doing, shucking corn, and just doing anything that came to mind.

Q   How long did you continue working for the Finks?

A   Since I was 10 years old until I was 25.

Q   Were you paid in 1938?

A   Maybe $500.00, but no special salary.

Q   Did his sister or mother give you any money?

A   About $10.00.

Q   How much in cash for your full years work?

A   Not over $50.00.

Q   When did you receive a salary?

A   In 1941 I received $225.00, 17 pounds of meat, and some flour.

Q   Was that a full year's salary?

A   Yes.

Q   Did Mr. Finks or your father ask you to pay any part of the $1200?

A   No.

Q   What did you consider you were working for?

A   That property.

Q   When did you get married?

A   In 1941 and I left in 1943.

Q   Were you paid a salary from 1941 to 1943?

A   Yes.

Q Did he say anything about whether you had paid him back for the $1200?

A No.

Q Did your father ever ask you anything about it?

A No.

Q How did you consider you bought it?

A Out of my labor. From the time I was 10 years old until I was 25 years old.

MR. ROBINSON: May we introduce three papers, the first of which is a deed dated the 28th of November, 1936, from Effie Diedrich and husband, to Wilson Kilby. Respondent's Exhibit A. Effie Diedrich and Mollie Jenkins – which was an option to sell it. Respondent's Exhibit B. This paper I now offer is a deed of J. Ray Hudson, Trustee, dated October 10,1953. I ask that this be marked Respondent's Exhibit C.

  (The documents above referred to were received in evidence as Respondents Exhibits A, B, and C.)

I will show you these three papers and ask you whether you have ever seen them.

Q Have you ever seen them before?

A Mr. Finks gave them to me and my mother.

Q When?

A About 1936.

Q How long was it after this property was bought?

A About two weeks.

Q Did he give them to you at one time?

A They were in one envelope.

Q Who handed them to you?

A Mr. Finks.

Q Who was present?

A My mother.

Q Did Mr. Finks say anything to you when he handed them to you?

A He said to keep them.

Q Did you have your own private box?

A Yes. They stayed there until I married and moved away.

Q Wilson, you left in 1943?

A Yes, sir.

Q Why?

A I couldn't take care of my wife and two kids. Mr. Finks told me I could move up into that house if I wanted to.

Q Who was present?

A My wife and mother.

Q Did he ask you for any money at any time?

A No.

Q When did Mr.Finks or your father claim that the property belonged to him?

A I don't know. The definite proof I had was August 4, 1954.

Q Who came to see you?

A My father came and Mr. Finks was with him. They didn't come in together.

Q Have you ever seen or talked to your father separate and apart from Mr. Finks?

A Yes, at the annual meeting at Woodville.

Q Did you discuss this with him?

A Yes.

Q Did he tell you that he was claiming the property?

A He said he would like to have $400. He also said he wouldn't go unless I talked to Mr. Finks.

Q Since that time have you ever seen your father without Mr. Finks?

A No.

Q   Have you ever used the property or lived on it?

A   No.

Q   Have you ever collected rent?

A   No, I left that to my father. I thought if he could get anything out of it, let him.

Q   Where do you now work?

A   At the American Viscose-about 45 miles from here.

Q   Who did you think was getting the benefit from the property?

A   My father. He never drew more than $250 a year, and after I left home I had mercy for him. I thought I should give him some consideration.

Q   Has there ever been any dispute with your father?

A   No, not before this case came up.

Q   Have you ever paid taxes on the property?

A   For two years.

Q   Have you ever received tax bills?

A   In 1946 and this year.

Q   Do you know who sent the tax bills to you?

A   I don't know whether it was Mr. Finks or my father.

Q   Did you ever talk to your brother Charles about who owned the property?

A   Charles and myself wasn't raised alike. He slept in a room with Mr. P.M. Finks.

Q   You heard him testify about the property belonged to your father?

A   He was not correct.

Q   Did you ever tell anyone that the property belonged to your father?

A   No.

Q   Has your father ever claimed to you that the property belonged to him?

A   No.

That is all.

CROSS EXAMINATION

BY MR. FLETCHER:

Q   You say you were born in 1917?

A   Yes.

Q   After that time where did you eat your meals?

A   In the Finks home. I want you to understand that Miss Emma and others didn't furnish all the food. My mother furnished some.

Q   Your mother prepared the food and you ate it until the time you left the farm!

Q   You said you didn't get any money from the Finks. Where did you get your clothes?

A   From what my father gave me.

Q   You had everything everyone else had didn't you? You all live at the Finks and had only what you made?

A   I had only what they gave me.

Q   Didn't you get the same breakfast the others got?

A   It was rough food.

Q   You continued to work there until he asked you to stay?

A   Mr. Finks ate most of his meals at his mother's. I don't know that Mr. Finks was ever separated. He continued to eat there.

Q   Did he pay you your wages?

A   No. It came out of the Finks family. My mother bought beans, we picked berries and she made preserves. We also picked apples. The Finks didn't give us all the food.

Q   When did you first hear that Mr. Finks was going to get this land for you?

A   In 1935.

Q   When did you get it?

A   In 1936.

Q   What happened between that time?

A   I thought I was going to get it.

Q   Do you know where Mollie Jenkins was living at that time?

A   She lived at the place a while, but I don't remember just how long.

Q   Did she live there in 1936 when the property was sold?

A   She lived there quite awhile.

Q   The sale didn't go through until 1936. How did you know that the property was going to be sold if Mrs. Jenkins just got an option in 1936? You testified that the property was to be sold to you in 1935. You told Mr. Robinson that they agreed for you to have the property in 1935. What apples did you pick on the farm?

A   The three of them had an apple orchard over in Madison County and we picked them up.

Q   Do you know what the wage scale was in 1941?

A   It was up since 1929.

Q   Do you know whether it was out of line for these years?

A   I think so.

Q   During 1941-1943 were you deferred to work on the farm?

A   They said they would turn me in to the draft board.

Q   Was Mr. Finks your paymaster?

A   I stayed with Mr. Finks when he didn't have a cook and spent the night with him. He gave me some money but I don't remember how much, I was under the control of Miss Edith and Miss Emma. Mr. Finks had a share in the property.

Q   Miss Emma owned the property until she died, didn't she?

A   Yes, that is correct.

Q   Did you help with the survey?

A   I knew about it.

Q   Did you ever have a discussion with him as to how much you owed him?

A   No, he never said a word about it.

Q   If he was giving you the place, how do you account for your father putting $400 up?

A Just because he wanted to I guess. I gave Mr. Finks my father's bank book and I don't know how he got the money. The folks we were raised with didn't tell us about business. Dr. Eastland did.

Q You say no one ever instructed you in business unless.....

MR. ROBINSON: I object: That is just argumentative.

JUDGE SNEAD: Objection sustained.

A I could say that my father wasn't getting more than $225 a year.

Q You say you didn't know anything about business. Do you know what other people are getting?

A I never discussed it with them.

Q Do you say that Charles made a false statement when he said you had a conversation with him about ownership of the land?

A Yes.

Q You deny that you talked to him about it?

A I deny it.

Q When did Mr. Finks tell you could move into the property if you liked?

MR. ROBINSON: I object:

JUDGE SNEAD: Objection over-ruled.

MR. ROBINSON: Exception.

WILSON KILBY CONTINUES

A He said I could move there if I wanted to.

Q Did he need to do that if you claimed ownership?

A It wasn't necessary.

Q Did your father come to you and ask you to release the deed to the property?

A He said he wanted to talk to me. He said he had been running around with that foolish man and wanted me to sign some papers, I told him no.

Q Did he explain what he meant by "that foolish man"?

A No.

Q Did Mr. Finks owe you any money in 1936?

A He must have felt he did.

Q Did he have any reason to prefer you over any of the other employees?

A I would say yes. He didn't tell Charles what to do. Willie wasn't raised there. He was raised with my grandmother.

Q When did Willie leave?

A I don't remember.

That is all.

JUDGE SNEAD TO WILSON KILBY

Q Did Conner Jenkins come to you?

A Mr. Conner Jenkins said why didn't I tell him the property belonged to me.

Q What day was that?

A It was in 1954.

Q What were the circumstances under which you saw Conner Jenkins?

A After the subpoena I investigated to see Mr. Jenkins. I went to the property and Mr. Jenkins was there. I spoke to him, and he said he was sorry he was on the property. That was the first time he ever said anything to me.

Q Did he ask you to sell the property?

A I said I couldn't sell it at the time. There was a conjunction on it – I think that is the legal word—and I couldn't sell it. I didn't know who Conner Jenkins was until that day.

MR. FLETCHER:

Q How long had Mr. Jenkins been share-cropping?

A I couldn't answer.

Q Who was with you when you went to see Mr. Jenkins?

A Mr. Joshua Robinson.

Q What day was it in 1935 that Mr. Finks promised to get this property for you?

A I couldn't tell you.

That is all.

CATHERINE AUSBERRY KILBY

Was called as a witness, and being first duly sworn,
was examined and testified as follows:

DIRECT EXAMINATION

BY MR. ROBINSON:

Q Tell the jury your name.

A Catherine Ausberry Kilby.

Q You are the wife of James Wilson Kilby?

A Yes.

Q When were you married?

A In April, 1941.

Q After you were married where did you live?

A With my father. Then we moved to the Eastland Place, and lived there for two years. From there we moved to Culpepper.

Q Did you hear any conversations between P.M. Finks and your husband?

A Mr. Finks told me that the place belonged to Wilson and that John had $400 in it. The last August he said he wanted $1200. My husband said what about the six years hard work? Mr. Finks told him that it was his hard luck.

That is all.

CROSS EXAMINATION

BY MR. FLETCHER:

Q What was your name before marriage?

A Catherine Ausberry.

Q Do you know anything about the original transaction?

A No, I wasn't married then.

Q But you do state that you heard Mr. Finks tell your husband it was your husband's property?

A Yes.

Q   Why did Mr. Finks have to tell you to move in to the house?

A   Because I didn't like the neighborhood.

Q   You saw Mr. Finks in 1954 when he came over to see you. Was Uncle John with him.

A   He was in the car. He came over about the $1200.

Q   Why did he come if he admitted it was Wilson's place?

A   My husband said he wouldn't do it because he had worked there till 1943.

MR. ROBINSON: I object to this line of questioning. It is argumentative.

JUDGE SNEAD: Objection over-ruled.

MR. ROBINSON; Exception.

MR. FLETCHER CONTINUES CROSS EXAMINATION

Q   Did you inquire from Mr. Finks if in 1943 the place was yours?

A   I didn't ask him anything.

That is all.

ASHLEY CARPENTER

Was called as a witness, and being first duly sworn, was examined and testified as follows:

DIRECT EXAMINATION

BY MR. ROBINSON:

Q   Tell the jury your name and age.

A   Ashley Carpenter. I am 39 years old.

Q   Do you know P. M. Finks?

A   Yes.

Q   How long?

A   Since 1935.

Q   Are you acquainted with the property in controversy?

A   Yes.

Q   Have you ever had any conversation with Mr. Finks about
    that property?

A   Yes. I tried to rent it once back in 1947 or 1948.

Q   What did he say?

A   He said I would have to see Wilson before he could rent it.

No further questions.

MR. ROBINSON: May it please the court. The respondent rest its case.

RE-DIRECT EXAMINATION OF MR. FINKS

BY MR. FLETCHER:

Q   How long before this deed was made did you discuss it with anyone.

A   I don't think I discussed it with anyone.

Q   How long was it before you got the deed?

A   About a week.

Q   How long was it before you first learned it was for sale?

A   I guess a week.

Q   The deed was made in 1936. Did you know it was for sale in 1935?

A   No.

Q   Did you promise Wilson Kilby that you would get it for him if he
    didn't go to New York?

MR. ROBINSON: I object: He is leading the witness,

JUDGE SNEAD: Objection sustained.

MR, FLETCHER CONTINUES RE-DIRECT EXAMINATION

Q   Did you make any promise to Wilson Kilby regarding the purchase
of this property?

A   No.

Q   When did you first have a conversation with Wilson Kilby about
    this promise?

A   Never!

Q Who did you deed this property to?

A Uncle John.

A Did you have any conversation with Wilson Kilby or his wife in 1943 with respect to this farm?

A No.

Q Did you have any conversation just prior to their leaving for the farm of Eastland?

A No.

Q Did you offer to permit him to move to this house in 1943?

A No.

Q Did Ashley Carpenter attempt to rent this property?

A Yes.

Q Tell the jury about it.

A He came to me and asked me to rent it to him. I told him I wasn't renting it to anyone. He just made that stuff up.

Q Were you financially interested in the farm of your sister or mother?

A No.

A Did you go back and forth to Miss Edith's house to take your meals?

A No.

Q You didn't have to ask anyone to rent the property, is that correct?

A I never told Ashley Carpenter anything. He came to me to rent it and I never mentioned Wilson's name. I didn't have to ask anybody to rent this property.

Q Did you owe money to Wilson Kilby in 1936?

A I don't know what you mean.

Q Did you owe him any money for services performed?

A   No.

JUDGE SNEAD TO MR. FINKS:

Q   How did John Henry Kilby become obligated to you for $1200?

A   When he bought the place, he paid $400 and I paid $1200.

Q   You are familiar with notes are you not?

A   No, I didn't take any note.

Q   How did you expect to get the money?

A   He always pays up.

Q   You stated that you had this property put in James Wilson Kilby's name because you had a dispute with your sister and you didn't want her to think you were taking these people away from her. Did you have any understanding that this property was to come back to you? Did you ever ask him anything about it?

A   No.

Q   You are a businessman?

A   I think so.

(Whereupon the court and counsel retired to chambers where the following proceedings were had):

MR. ROBINSON: I renew the motion to strike the evidence on the grounds previously noted.

JUDGE SNEAD: over-ruled.

MR. ROBINSON: Exception.

MR. ROBINSON: Add to the grounds to strike, the defense of latches.

> (Whereupon instructions to the jury were prepared by court and counsel. Counsel for both sides made argument to the jury, following which the jury retired to consider its verdict.)

> (Whereupon, at 4:30 p.m., the trial of the above-captioned case was concluded.)

"The court instructs the jury that where upon the purchase of property, the conveyance of legal title is taken in the name of one person, while the consideration or part thereof is paid by another, the parties being strangers (that is to say not near relatives or persons for whom the purchaser is under an obligation to provide) a resulting trust immediately arises from the transaction and the person named as grantee in the conveyance is a trustee for the party from whom the consideration proceeded, however, in the case of the conveyance to a child, no such presumption arises as on the contrary a presumption of a gift or advance to the child arises. This presumption of a gift or advancement is a presumption of fact and not law and may be rebutted by parole evidence or circumstances showing a contrary intention.

The court then proceeded to instruct the jury, and submitted the following questions:

"Did John Henry Kilby pay of obligate himself to pay all of the consideration for land described in the case?"

Did the parties intend that the land in question be deed to James Wilson Kilby as a gift or transfer for service, or was it intended that the land should be held by James Wilson Kilby for John Henry Kilby?"

The jury retired to consider its verdict.

They returned quickly.

In response to the first question, the jury answered "yes." In response to the second question, the jury answered, "It was intended that the land should be held by James Wilson Kilby for John Henry Kilby." The decision had been pronounced by the jury. It was over. The jury started leaving the jury box.

According to Daddy, after the jury was discharged, his attorney moved the Court to set aside the findings of the jury as contrary to the law and evidence. The judge over-ruled that motion. Then he requested a ruling upon the plea of laches filed in this cause. The judge over-ruled this motion as well. In just one day, it was all over. White Judge, and an all white jury had taken my land from me. The judge ordered and decreed that I turn over the deed and all claims to the property. In a separate order he ordered and decreed the same thing to Momma. It was never about the land. I had already bought 52 acres in Happy Creek. It was about being a MAN. It was a symbol of justice. There was no justice for this Negro. It was about the Kilbys owning something as a family. Why did he wait so long? Would the devastation have been any different had he taken the land shortly after I left the farm? Why didn't he try to take the land while my mother was still living? Would I have lost if I were better educated? The answers did not come, my only thought was, my father betrayed me, my children and my children's children for old man Dick Finks, the man he saw as his master. One of the jurors, Rhodes Brown, a white man, refused to serve saying, "This is not right. Is the law justice?" Rhodes had honor. That was stealing and he was aware of it. Daddy continued to tell us, "My own father betrayed me, his son, for old man Dick Finks. How could this man be so evil, he took my mother, he took my sister, he took my land and he took my father. I wondered how so much could have been lost in just one action."

There was always pain and hurt when he talked about losing his land. Daddy refused to hand the deed over to either Granddaddy John or old man Dick Finks, therefore, a Special Commissioner was appointed to execute and deliver a deed conveying with Special Warranty of Title of Daddy's twenty-four acres. On February 14, 1956, Granddaddy got the deed to the property. On March 29, 1956, Granddaddy John deeded the property to old man Dick Finks. The deed said, "for ten dollars in consideration." It was clearly evident that they all lied in court.

Daddy was never really the same after that court battle. During the years that followed, he would dictate a cover letter to my brothers and then to me as I got older. He would say, "I was robbed of my land by a white judge and an all white jury. The judicial system doesn't work when I, a colored man, had legal papers showing ownership of land for my hard work. It was taken from me." We sent that transcript of the trail to several presidents, and most of the Virginia senators and delegates. As we were gathering information to document my father's life, we found a response to a letter that Daddy wrote to John Edgar Hoover:

United Stated Department of Justice
Federal Bureau of Investigation
Washington 12, D.C.
July 11, 1956

Mr. J.W. Kilby
Happy Creek, Virginia

Dear Mr. Kilby:

Your letter postmarked July 5, 1956 has been received, and it is
suggested that you communicate with my representatives located at
501 Southern State Building, Richmond 17, Virginia if you believe
you possess facts relating to any matter within the investigative
jurisdiction of the FBI.

> Sincerely yours,
> John Edgar Hoover
> Director

Sometimes we would receive a response, saying that there was nothing
that could be done. Sometimes, we would be referred to someone else.
Nothing changed. I grew-up to understand my father's spirit of never giving
up. Even at eighty-three years old, Daddy still refers to that piece of land as
his land.

Daddy was always driven, but after he lost his 24 acres of land in Peola
Mills, he was focused, hell-bent and determined to make our farm in
Happy Creek a successful business. He was equally determined that we
were going to get an education. He would whip us if we did not make good
grades on our report card or there was a notation that we were acting up in
school. Sick or well, we went to school.

Chapter 3————————————————————

Death of Innocence

I woke up alone on the stage floor behind the curtain,
exposed and violated. I got up, removed the tape from
my mouth and went to the girl's restroom.

*D*uring Negro History Week 1958, Daddy invited Rev. Frank, a local
minister and teacher at Johnson-Williams High School, to speak at the
Ressie Jeffries Elementary School PTA meeting. Rev. Frank talked about
Oliver Brown, a Negro resident of Topeka, Kansas, who wanted his eight-
year-old daughter, Carol Ann, admitted to a white school. Rev. Frank told the
group that, on May 17, 1954, the Supreme Court gave its verdict in the case
of *Oliver Brown, et al vs. Board of Education of Topeka.* In handing down
his decision, Justice Warren said, "In the field of public education, the old
doctrine of separate but equal has no place, separate educational facilities
are inherently unequal, therefore, we hold that the plaintiffs are, by reason
of segregation complained of, deprived of the equal protection of the laws
as guaranteed by the Fourteenth Amendment." Rev. Frank discussed the
disadvantages of the segregated system stating that, "Negro children
graduating from Johnson-Williams High School in Berryville and Manassas
Regional High School in Manassas had an education two or three years
behind their white counterparts." I heard Daddy on the phone saying,
"Justice Warren said that separate educational facilities was unequal and Rev.
Frank was right when he said that our children had an education two or
three years behind their white counterparts." He got up in church on Sunday
morning and talked about Rev. Frank's message at the PTA meeting. Daddy
said that Rev. Frank's message was right in line with the October and
December 1957 PTA meetings where Mr. and Mrs. John Jackson, Mr. and
Mrs. Mack Jackson, Mr. and Mrs. John Groves and Mrs. Pearl Jordan, had
signed the petition expressing their desire for their high school children to
remain in the county for the 1958–1959 school term.

In late April and early May, parents were required to sign Pupil Placement forms indicating where they wanted to send their children to high school. I couldn't understand why my dad wasn't like everyone else's dad when it came to those Pupil Placement forms. I was not the first child in our family to go to high school. I remembered the year before when it was time to sign the Pupil Placement form for my brother Bubble; Daddy wasn't satisfied. My brother Jimmy went to boarding school in Manassas when he finished elementary school. Daddy wasn't happy because Jimmy got in trouble stealing milk and lost his weekend bus privilege for one month. That meant that Jimmy either couldn't come home or Daddy had to make transportation arrangements for Jimmy to come home on the weekends after his privileges were suspended. Daddy needed Jimmy to help with the farm. Jimmy told Daddy that the big boys took his money and if they wanted something on his food tray they took what they wanted. Jimmy told Daddy that he was hungry most of the time. He was also scared of the big boys who picked on him. Daddy went to Manassas for a parent teacher conference. The school officials told Daddy that since he lived outside of Prince Williams County he didn't have a voice. Manassas Regional High School was located in Prince Williams County, Virginia. Daddy went to the Warren County School Board to complain about the school in Manassas and his inability to have a voice in a school system where his son was being educated. Daddy put up such a fight, he got Jimmy's bus privileges restored, in fact, Jimmy was allowed to come home every weekend after the incident. Daddy ranted and raved for weeks and vowed to Jimmy that he would not have to go back to Manassas the next school year. When Daddy complained that Johnson-Williams was not on the Pupil Placement form that Bubble brought home, the school board added Johnson-Williams in Berryville, Virginia, to the Pupil Placement form right away. I thought Daddy would be happy to send me to Johnson-Williams with my brothers.

I asked Daddy every night for two weeks to sign my Pupil Placement form. Every time I reminded him that Mrs. Jeffries kept asking me for that form he would get mad. I thought that I was doing something wrong. One night, I began to cry when Daddy did not give me the form back. Then he handed me the form. I could see that he had marked through the school names and wrote in Warren County High School (WCHS). I knew I was going to be in trouble because Mrs. Jeffries didn't like messy papers. The next morning I handed the paper to Mrs. Jeffries and she looked mad then she asked, "Did you do this?" "No ma'am," I replied. She said, "Your father messed up this form." She tore up the form and threw it in the trash can, and gave me another form. That night I gave the form to Daddy. I told Daddy that Mrs. Jeffries said that he messed up the form. I told him, "Mrs. Jeffries said you should circle either Johnson-Williams or Manassas High School, sign the form and you should not write anything on this paper." I was shocked when Daddy did it again. He scratched out the options and wrote Warren County High School. The next day I wasn't anxious to get fussed at, so I told Mrs. Jeffries that I forgot the form. I was hoping that she would forget it too. I sat in the corner fussing to myself, "Why don't my Daddy just do what he was supposed to do?" He made me live in the country and the town kids made fun of me. He made me live on the farm and even the other kids from Happy Creek called us "cow horses." He let us be poor because the other kids had store-bought white bread and their sandwiches were wrapped with wax paper. We had biscuits with sausage wrapped with brown paper bags. The other kids had lunch boxes but Momma used half the grocery sack to wrap our biscuits and the other half of the sack served as our lunch box. I just wanted to be like the town kids but my Daddy wouldn't let me be like everyone else. No, not my Daddy! When Mrs. Jeffries threatened to call my Daddy, I found the form and gave it to her. I knew she wouldn't be happy with Daddy or me. She tore up that form and gave me another one. This time she was really mad when she said, "I want you to tell your Daddy that this is the last time I am sending this form to him and I want him to do it right this time." When Daddy came up from the barn, just the thought of the fire in Mrs. Jeffries eyes made me weak at the knees. This time I opened the form up and put it in Daddy's plate at the dinner table. Daddy asked, "Why is this paper in my plate?" I told him that I was afraid that Mrs. Jeffries was going to be mad so I didn't give her the form right away. I began to cry. Then I relayed Mrs. Jeffries's message. Boy was he mad! To my surprise he did it again. He scratched out his options so hard that he put a hole in the paper. Then he handed me the paper. He said, "Don't you be afraid. You give this paper to Mrs. Jeffries tomorrow and you tell her this is the last time that I am going to send this form to her. Tell her to call me if she doesn't like what is on the paper." I truly forgot to give Mrs. Jeffries the form right away.

The next morning during roll call Mrs. Jeffries asked for the form. As I stood up to take the form to her I said out loud for all the world to hear including "Old Mrs. Fandanahan" the truant officer, who was visiting our school that day, "My Daddy said that this is the last time that he is sending this form to you and if you don't like what is on the paper you call my Daddy." All the kids in the class laughed. Wow, I had sassed the teacher right in front of "Old Mrs. Fandanahan" and I was a hero to the town kids that day. They patted me on the back all day and treated me like I was one of their friends. That night after dinner the phone rang, I answered it, "This is Mrs. Fandanahan from the School Board Office, is Mr. Kilby there?" I said, "yes" and handed the phone to Daddy. I heard Daddy say, "This is Kilby, yes I did. Your form asked where I want to send Betty to high school. Well in 1956 I sent my son James to Manassas to the boarding school. Sixty miles away was too far even if it is only a weekly commute; and besides, James was too young to be away from home. He was just a little shy farm boy that the big boys picked on. Manassas didn't work for Jimmy or me. In 1957, I sent James and John to Berryville. Berryville was a 60 miles a day trip with the school bus picking my sons up at 6 AM and sometimes they didn't return until 7 or 7:30 PM. My boys had to walk half a mile to meet the "colored bus, while the bus carrying white kids drove past my boys walking. The bus ran into the potholes in the road and splashed water, mud and snow on James and John. John developed sinus problems. The bus constantly broke down, they were getting in at all hours of the night, there was no supervision on the bus, several girls got pregnant and I will not subject my daughter to such conditions. I wasn't satisfied with that option either. You don't have to subject your kids to this kind of environment to get an education and I will not subject my kids to this kind of environment any more. You have the form. I wrote in my option of Warren County High School. "If you don't like it you can just lump it." My Daddy was mad. I had never heard him talk this way before. It seemed as though he didn't even breathe in between the sentences. He hung up the phone. I heard the voices coming from Momma and Daddy's bedroom that night, Momma said, "Kilroy you are going to keep on messing around with these white folks, somebody is going to get hurt." Daddy said, "Catherine, get ready for a fight because Betty ain't going to Manassas or Berryville, she is going to Warren County High School. Don't you remember what Rev. Frank said about separate not being equal? Besides, we are not alone. John Jackson is going to turn in a form tomorrow to send his daughter Barbara to WCHS too."

While school was in session, Daddy picked up trash from Warren County High School. He would bring the trash home on the back of his truck. Pat, Gene and I would unload the truck and separate the trash while Daddy, Jimmy and Bubble milked the cows. We threw the paper in the barrel that we used to burn the trash and the foodstuff in the container for the hogs. Sometimes, Daddy would pick me up at school and take me with him when he went to the high school to pick up trash. I liked going with him because I got to spend time with my Daddy. Daddy was always carrying the boys around with him, but for me it was special. He would ask, "Do you like this school?" Naturally, I would say "yes." Daddy would say, "You are going to this school this fall," I asked, "What about Johnson-Williams?" I could see the blood vessels in his forehead swelling and I knew Daddy wasn't happy with that response. He would ask, "What do you want to be when you grow up?" He suggested that I should be a teacher. I loved the attention, so I got excited about going to Warren County High School and becoming a teacher.

Daddy was President of the Parents Teachers Association (PTA). Daddy told me that the PTA voted to give the top five children in my class $5.00 for graduation. They used the five highest scores from the test that determined whether children passed the seventh grade. He said that if I was in the top five of my class of twenty-seven that he would give me another $5. Momma said that she would give me some Queen Ann shoes (shoes with 1-inch heels) for graduation. I studied real hard over the next couple of months, always doing my homework and paying attention in class because I wanted that $10 and Queen Ann shoes. Most of the girls in my class were getting high heels and were going to wear stockings for the first time. I prayed that my test scores would be in the top five. The day the test scores were posted, I was afraid to look. The highest score was 11.5; 11.0 then 10.5 three times, Jerome Jackson, William Williams and I scored 10.5. I made the top five's list. I jumped for joy and I thanked God because I had prayed so much. I wanted that $10 and my shoes, but most of all, I wanted to be that special little girl, just for a little while. The last time I remembered being the special child was when I had an allergic reaction to something in the nut family and got a rash all over my body. I was in the hospital for two weeks and I had to take a shot in the butt every day. Momma and Daddy came to see me every night and bought me candy and oranges. Daddy would say "How's my girl tonight?"

My graduation day finally came and Momma not only gave me heels; she bought me stockings, a new dress and the prettiest crinoline slip. The slip had a tier representing all the colors of the rainbow. It was far too pretty to go under the dress. When we took our class pictures, I crossed my legs so everyone could see my pretty slip and I held my five-dollar bill next to my diploma. That was one of the happiest days of my life.

Daddy joined the National Association for the Advancement of Colored People (NAACP). He also convinced Charles and Pearl Dean, Sam and Estelle Fletcher, Henretta Baltimore, Sara Jackson, Bessie Pines, Viola and Russell Coleman, Anne Rhodes, Nellie Lewis, Enoch Love, Charles and Thelma Washington, John and Pauline Jackson and Phyllis Grier to join. Shortly after joining the NAACP, Daddy and a committee from the NAACP went to Richmond to consult with Oliver W. Hill and retain Mr. Hill as legal advisor. Mr. Hill wrote a letter to the Warren County School Board on behalf of the these Warren County families to enroll twenty-four Negro children in the Warren County High School, and five Negro children in the Warren County Elementary School stating: "In view of the fact, as of the end of the school year 1957-1958, you were maintaining and operating the public schools under your jurisdiction upon a basis of racial segregation, I request that on or before July 21, 1958, I be advised as to whether or not the requested transfers be honored." The request was placed on the school board agenda for August 14, 1958. Shortly after Oliver Hill sent the letter to the school board, it was announced in local newspapers that the school board was excepting bids, for the construction of the new colored high school, to be built on Criser Road in Front Royal and scheduled to open in September 1959. By this time our parents involved in the request were no longer interested in separate educational facilities, they realized that separate educational facilities would never be equal. Daddy said, "White supremacy had existed too long, they deliberately attempt to keep the Negro uneducated."

One of my elementary teachers and family friend, Mrs. Irby, invited me to go to Blackstone, Virginia, with her for summer vacation. I asked if Barbara Jackson could come too and Mrs. Irby invited Barbara too. Even though Barbara was only a couple of months older than me she was much more mature. Barbara also dressed more mature. One of the big outings in Blackstone was the Tobacco Festival. Mrs. Irby took her family, Barbara and me to the Tobacco Festival. Barbara wanted to dress grown up so she let me wear one of her outfits. The halter-top that she let me wear was too big. I stuffed the cup with athletic socks and it made me look like I had a really big chest. Mrs. Irby asked, "Do your parents let you girls dress like that? We said, "Yes! These are the only casual clothes we brought with us." She bought our story and didn't make us change. A lot the big boys were flirting with Barbara and me. Our male suitors bought us hot dogs and sodas. I had such a good time.

I played the "cake walk" game. It cost ten cents. The players walked around stepping on squares as the music played, when the music stopped, the moderator called out the winning number, if you were standing on the winning square you won the cake. After about five tries, I won! I chose the five-layer coconut cake. We took the cake home and shared it with the Irby family.

The Saturday night church service was also a part of the Festival. The boys invited us to the church service and asked if we would sit with them in church. To keep up our grown-up appearance Barbara let me borrow a pair of her stockings, however, she only had one pair of garters to hold up the stockings. Naturally, she used the garters. She taught me how to roll the top of the stockings and make a knot to hold up the stockings; then tie a scarf around the top of the stockings. This method only worked temporarily. When I walked up to put my money in the collection plate my stockings and the bright colored scarf fell to my ankles. I kept on walking out the door. As soon as I got to a private area, I took off the stockings. On the way home from church, Mrs. Irby asked, "Betty, how did that scarf work on those stockings?" I stumbled for words. Then she said, "You youngsters haven't been around the cup far enough to find the handle." Barbara looked at me and I looked at her, we knew we were caught and if that was the punishment, it wasn't so bad.

Mr. Irby took us to the tobacco field and gave us a lesson on harvesting and curing tobacco. I was fascinated with the tobacco because it was the first time that I saw a tobacco plant. Mr. Irby gave Barbara and me a couple of leaves to take home. I took my tobacco home and hung it in the closet just like it was hanging in the tobacco barn. When it had dried sufficiently, I crushed it on a sheet of notebook paper. I rolled and licked the last roll like I saw uncle John do when he rolled his cigarettes. It didn't stay together like Uncle John's cigarette so I glued my cigarette with Elmer's glue. I had the longest cigarette in the world. I sat in the comfort chair in my room and lit up the cigarette. I got a couple of puffs in before the cigarette caught on fire. I was able to throw the cigarette in the stove before I caught on fire. I didn't want to get caught with that tobacco smell in my room so I opened the window and tried to fan the smoke out the window. I decided that I should leave the room. I started for the stairs. I was dizzy, I stepped wrong and fell down the stairs. I got sick to my stomach. I was sick for two days.

I was able to convince Momma that it must have been something that I ate. I had no desire to smoke after that. I called Barbara and warned her that the tobacco would make her sick.

On July 19, 1958, the news hit the front page of the *Northern Virginia Daily*, "NAACP Launches Surprise Desegregation Attack on Front Royal School." *Betty Kilby et als, Plaintiffs vs. The County School Board of Warren County, Virginia* and *Q. D. Gasque, Division Superintendent of School for Warren County Virginia*, Defendants to admit twenty-four Negro children in the Warren County High School, and five Negro children in the Warren County Elementary School was filed in the Fifth United States District Court for Western Virginia, Harrisonburg, Virginia. Virginia Governor Stanley called a special session of the General Assembly, a session devoted to creating the legal framework of Massive Resistance. The Governor told the legislators that he could not "recommend any legislations, or actions, which accepts the principle of integration of the races in the public schools." At a large picnic function at his Berryville orchard, Senator Byrd announced that, "Virginia must fight with every ounce of energy and capacity. Let Virginia surrender to this illegal demand, you'll find the ranks of the South will go down too."

We were talked about on the front page of the *Northern Virginia Daily* again on July 24, 1958 in an article titled, "Warren Citizens Calm and Concerned." Several citizens were interviewed for their reaction of the Negro's request to enter the Warren County's white schools. The opinion of white citizens interviewed were that the schools should not be closed. According to the *Northern Virginia Daily*, the survey showed that race relations in Front Royal and Warren County "have always been good and citizens both white and colored wanted it to continue that way." Good, I thought. How good could race relations be? Old man Dick Finks took Daddy's land, that wasn't good. Colored men were still being lynched, that wasn't good. It wasn't that long ago that I heard them talking about Clarence Dearing being put in jail for refusing to work on a farm in Rappahannock County. Relationships were good as long as colored folks followed orders and accepted things. Well, anyway, a young white woman, Virginia born and reared secretary, a June graduate of Warren County High School said she favors integration stating, "It is a shame that those kids (colored) have to go to Berryville and Manassas to school." A white manager of a Front Royal business firm thinks the colored citizens should have waited another year stating, "We are going to build them a school, and it would have been ready for the beginning of the 1959 term. I think they should have waited and I believe the colored of Warren County would have waited if outsiders would have minded their own business." A white Warren County High School senior says, "I feel sorry for the students that have to travel so far to school. They have a reasonable gripe, but I do wish they would have waited until the new school was built." One white housewife reports that, "I am in favor of separate schools but the main concern now is to keep the schools open. I have a daughter that will enter the first grade this year, and I would rather see integration than see trouble at the schools." A few of the people interviewed were not concerned at all about the situation and had no comment to make on the problem.

The colored (as we were called back then) folks had opinions too, except the news reporter didn't reflect the "colored opinion" or they just didn't bother to put the opinion of colored folks in that article. Most of the reports were meant to divide the Negroes. The newspaper reported any attempt Negro or white to convince the Negro participants seeking admittance to WCHS to withdraw their petition. The colored opinions were as varied as the opinions of the white folks. Enoch Love who was an original petitioner withdrew the names of his children because he was happy with the option of sending his children to the proposed Criser School. Daddy received calls both civil and threatening from concerned white and colored folks asking him to withdraw our petition to integrate the schools because they were concerned for the safety of the colored citizens of Warren County. We were caught in the middle of this war of integration.

Daddy told Momma that some of the guys at work told him that Front Royal and our case was in the television (TV) news. He wanted to know what she thought about buying a TV so that we could stay informed. We were all delighted over the prospect of getting a TV. Most of our friends already had a TV. That Saturday morning after Daddy and the boys finished milking the cows, we had breakfast, cleaned up the kitchen, bathed and changed into our street clothes; we all loaded into the car and went to town. We went to Kibler Furniture store and bought a 21-inch black and white screen TV. That Saturday evening we watched the news and "Amos and Andy." "Amos and Andy" was a show with colored characters.

Early the morning of August 21, 1958 the phone started ringing. There was an article in the *Northern Virginia Daily* newspaper titled, "Request Denied To Admit Negro School Pupils." The article included the complete text of the letter authorized by the school board sent to our lawyer, Oliver W. Hill, responding to Oliver's letters. The letter was dated August 14, 1958, signed by Q.D. Gasque the Virginia Pupil Placement Board was copied. The letter read as follows:

Dear Mr. Hill:

The Warren County School Board held its regular meeting today and your letters of July 3rd, and 23rd and August 13, were brought to their attention. The request that you made on behalf of your clients has had the very careful study and consideration of the Board insofar as limited time has been available. The Board has authorized me to advise you that we regard the power to enroll and place children in public schools of Warren County as vested in the Virginia Pupil Placement Board, under and by virtue of Paragraph 22-232.1 of the Code of Virginia as, amended, and your letter and Placement applications made by your clients have been forwarded to that Board.

It is the recommendation of the Warren County School Board to the Pupil Placement Board that it deny the request of your clients to be transferred to Warren County High School and Front Royal Elementary School, on a number of grounds, including the following:

1. Your request for transfer was made on behalf of your clients whom you represent to be 15 parents representing 11 families, and their 30 children. We find that of this number all who were required to sign pupil placement forms, with the exception of two parents involving only two children, have made in their own handwriting, written request to the Pupil Placement Board for assignment to a public school, either without specifying the name or location of the school or specifying their desire to have their children enrolled in the Johnson-Williams School of Berryville, Virginia, or the Manassas Regional School, Manassas, Virginia.

2. The Warren County High School is presently so over-crowded that it could not accommodate the applicants represented by you without seriously taxing the capacity of that school and a further lowering of the efficiency of the course of instruction offered there. For the session of 1957-58, the school Board enrolled 1062 students, which is 222 in excess of the number the high school building can properly accommodate. There will be no reduction in this enrollment for the current year.

3. The Front Royal Elementary School is presently so overcrowded that it could not accommodate the applicants represented by you without seriously taxing the capacity of that school and a further lowering of the efficiency of the course of instruction offered there. For the session 1957-58 the school board enrolled 1328 students which is 293 in excess of the number the elementary school building can properly accommodate. Also all sections of grades 1 and 2, eight in number, were operated last year on a one-half day basis and must be operated this year on a like basis. No reduction in this year

For your further information, all pupils who have been enrolled in the Warren County High School for the session 1958-59 have already been assign to home rooms and classes. It would be virtually impossible "to squeeze in" any additional pupils. As a matter of fact, certain classes, such as home economics, industrial arts, typing and band have already been filled to the point where it has become necessary to reject request from parents desiring to enroll their children in such courses.

4. The School Board of Warren County has authorized the construction of a new high and elementary school in the town of Front Royal in this county. When the school is completed, the additional physical facilities so provided will enable the Pupil Placement Board and the school board to enroll your clients in a public school in Warren County. It is expected that this will be ready for occupancy by September 1959.

5. The school board did not anticipate any request from the Negro residents of Warren County to desegregate the school of the county for the 1958-59 session. In view of the many complexities, problems and dislocations that are presented by such a request.

6. To grant the request of your clients for assignment to the Warren County High School and the Front Royal Elementary School for the session 1958-59 would not be in their interest or in the interest of other children in the county or the people of the county. Aside from the impelling reasons listed above, such assignments at this time and under conditions and circumstances presently existing could easily disrupt the entire school system of the county.

The Warren County School Board will need time to consider the full import of your request and to assess, appraise and evaluate its impact on Warren County and its people. For the board to take precipitate action could be ill-advised, and could be attended by disastrous consequences.

Barbara called me on the telephone and asked, "What does the article in the paper mean? Do you think our parents will send just the two of us to WCHS since we were the only two children of the two families who signed the Pupil Placement forms with Warren County High School?" I told her my Daddy really wanted me to go to WCHS real bad and that if he had the chance he would make me go even if it meant that I went by myself. We read excerpts from the article hoping that we would all be denied so the two of us wouldn't have to go to WCHS.

Daddy finally got home from work. Momma told Daddy, "The phone was ringing off the hook today." She asked, "What does it mean?" Daddy said, "Just like there was no room for Baby Jesus in Bethlehem, these folks are saying there is no room for our children in the white Warren County School System." I guess that meant that Daddy wasn't going to say anything in front of us kids. Momma and Daddy's bedroom was next door to the kitchen and I heard them talking that night and I heard Daddy say, "We are going to court. We got law on our side and Oliver W. Hill is one smart Negro. As hard as the white man tried to keep us uneducated, they failed. Old man Dick Finks kept me uneducated and he succeeded but this is the last generation of dumb Kilbys."

During July and August, we made numerous trips to Harrisonburg for court. I didn't pay close attention to what was going on in the courtroom. I was more interested in talking to my new white friend Ann Marx. Ann had long, straight blond hair and blue eyes but she looked like those white people that hated us but she wasn't like them. Ann's mother was one of the people working with the NAACP and our families to help us get in school. She had a good heart.

During lunch recess the first day that we went to court, Ann decided that we should go to lunch at a restaurant. As we walked to lunch we discussed what we were going to order. We found a restaurant that looked good. We walked in and sat in a booth. The man walked over and said, "You can stay (pointing to Ann) the rest of them Niggers got to go." Ann said, "We will all go! We didn't want your old food anyway." As we walked out the door the man yelled, "Nigger lover." On the way back to the courthouse, we went into a convenience store and bought junk food. Ann told her mother what happened. As our drivers dropped each one of us off at our house, our parents were instructed to pack our lunch the next time we went to court. That night Momma told Daddy what happened to us when we went to the restaurant. Daddy said to us, "This is why you are in court, to gain admittance to Warren County High School. For a long as you have a substandard education the white folks are going to treat you like Niggers." Daddy sat us down at the kitchen table and said, "Someday, you are going to have a good education, a good job or you may be working for yourself and you are going to have plenty of money. You be strong and keep on praying for these white folks because they don't know it yet but we ain't gonna let nobody turn us around." After that first day, we would aim to get to the courthouse early so that we could park close to the shaded area where we could have lunch in or around the cars. Mrs. Butler provided a cooler with water and sodas. It got pretty hot in Harrisonburg, Virginia, during the month of August. We made haste in eating and getting back to the air-conditioned courthouse. One day as we sat in the heat having our lunch, I told the group, "Someday, we are going to have a good education, a good job or you maybe own our own restaurant and we are going to have plenty of money. You just watch and see."

All the other Warren County school children white and colored started back to school for the 1958-1959 school session except Barbara, my brothers and me. I cried when the bus went past our house and didn't stop. I called Barbara and we cried together. I told Barbara, "I can't believe that my Daddy wouldn't let me go to school. He would whip my butt if I didn't make good grades, now he is going to make me get behind in my grades." My friend, Alease, went to William C. Taylor in Warrenton. She called me when she came from school to tell me that she met my cousins at school. I was happy for her but I wasn't happy about missing my high school experience.

On September 4, 1958, Federal Judge John Paul told Warren County School Board Officials that they could not deny Negroes admission to the county's only high school because of race. He instructed the attorneys to have an order ready for his signature on Monday, September 8, 1958, to have the twenty-two high school students admitted to the Warren County High School. The reaction to Judge Paul's decision was no longer calm but concerned.

Early Thursday morning September 11, we went to Baltimore. Chief Judge Simon E. Sabloff of the U.S. Fourth Circuit Court of Appeals refused to grant a stay of the desegregation order while it was being appealed. Attorney Hill spoke to Commonwealth Attorney W. J. Phillips after court and was told that upon return to Front Royal, the twenty-two Negro children would be allowed to enroll for the high school at the office of Superintendent Q. D. Gasque on Saturday and Monday.

The next morning, September 12, 1958, the headlines in the local newspaper said, "Warren County High School Suspends Classes." The school board issued these two statements: "In order for the Warren County School Board to have an opportunity to properly review the applications of the infant plaintiffs for enrollment in Warren County High School, the classes have been temporarily suspended as of the closing of said school on Friday, September 12, 1958. Applicants desiring to enroll in Warren County High School will be required to report to the superintendent of school's office in the Warren County Court House to make application. The registration will be held during regular office hours on Saturday, September 13, 1958 and Monday, September 15, 1958."

According to the *Northern Virginia Daily*, the students of Warren County showed mixed emotions as the school closed, some were in tears, others expressed or showed no emotion, most of them said they were anti-integrationists. Mike Berryman, president of the senior class said that in his opinion, the majority of the student body preferred segregation, but would make the best of an integrated school, "I believe that most of us would integrate rather than see the school closed." Mike added, "In one sense I don't think its exactly fair for twenty-two to hold back 1100 of us from getting an education. There are a few bad ones who might make trouble but I believe the rest of us could make them behave. We believe we could ignore them (the Negro students) and go on as we always have." Deanna Turner, a 12th grader, said "I hate to see it integrated; if it is, then they'll take over the restaurants and everything else." Charles Harrison a senior, said he favors equal facilities for Negro students but not integrated ones. "They are going to have a better high school than ours," referring to the Negro combined elementary and high school under construction. The last event of the day was a pep rally, customary before a football game. Warren County had played its first football game of the season the night before. Just as Mike Berryman had said, "We can ignore the Negroes and go on just as we always have," they did precisely that.

We had a NAACP meeting that Friday night. On the way to the NAACP meeting, Daddy drove past the school and there was a "NO TRESPASSING" sign erected at the front entrance to the high school. Attorney Hill gave us the inside story. Despite the statement in the paper, Attorney Hill told us that he did not believe the school board would allow us to register for Warren County High School on Saturday morning but we were going to try anyway. At this point all of the high school kids involved in the case were out of school. We went over the plans for Saturday, the designated drivers, what to expect, meeting times, schedule and how to respond to the media. He was so together and impressive. Our first stop was at the school board office. Q.D. Gasque informed us that we could not enroll for high school. Then we went to the Warren County Courthouse as planned. We filled out the registration papers. Mrs. Marx and Mrs. Whitted worked with us on filling out applications. As instructed we took our time to avoid making mistakes, wrote legible so that the authorities could understand our writing and filled in all the blanks. The younger kids were told to pair up with the older kids so that the older kids could review the younger kids applications. Just as we were instructed, we acted as though we were small soldiers, standing tall, proud and dignified with no talking or complaining.

Oliver Hill was feeling quite confident. Now that Attorney Hill had the attention of the press and the local citizens, he spoke boldly and confidently, "The situation is deplorable. I propose to use every legal means I can to make the schools available to white and colored. I believe if the people of Warren County were allowed to use their Constitutional Right, there would be no problem in Warren County." Daddy's eyes glowed as he pushed out his chest and smiled with satisfaction when Attorney Hill spoke. He would say, "If the Finks had let me go to school, I could have been just like Oliver W. Hill and I wouldn't have lost my land." I was confused! Daddy, Attorney Hill and the other parents were joyful. We didn't get registered in school, us kids still wasn't going to school. I couldn't see no joy. All I knew was, our leaders kept telling us the eyes of the world were upon us and we had to act like we were in church all the time and nobody was going to high school in Warren County. My friend Alease would call me and tell me all about high school and I just got depressed. I started having this recurring dream that I was going to school but I was lost. I couldn't find my classrooms, I couldn't find my class schedule and I couldn't find my locker. I would end up running for the bus and I missed the bus, too. I would wake up feeling stupid because I wasn't in school. Integration, segregation, all I wanted was an education.

Under Virginia law, the assignment or enrollment of any Negro pupil to a white school automatically forces that school to close. The state took over closing the schools under the Massive Resistance Law issuing this statement from Virginia's Governor Almond. "Under the compulsion of an order issued by the United States District Court for the Western District of Virginia, both white and colored children have been enrolled effective September 15, 1958, in the Warren County High School, located in the County of Warren. Pursuant of the provisions of Chapter 9.1 of the code of Virginia, the Warren County High School is closed and is removed from the public school system, effective September 15, 1958, and all authority, power and control over such school, its principal, teachers, other employees and all pupils now enrolled or ordered to be enrolled, will thereupon be vested in the Commonwealth of Virginia, to be exercised by the governor." The case in Warren County was the first school to be tested under the Massive Resistance laws. The eyes of the world were on Warren County and this case. No sooner than Governor Almond made the announcement, Governor Orval Faubus of Little Rock, Arkansas, followed suit in closing Little Rock High School that had been integrated in 1957 by the "Little Rock Nine."

Anticipating the next move by the NAACP to challenge the constitutionality of the school closure law under which Governor Almond acted, the State asked the Virginia Supreme Court for a ruling on the legality of the school closure law enacted in 1956. State officials believed that no federal court would be comfortable to consider a law while it was under consideration by a state court. This move would buy time for the lawyers to prepare their cases since the next court session did not open until October 6.

Within a month the white students were attending classes funded by a private education committee, The Warren County Educational Foundation. According to Rebecca Poe, a news reporter for the *Northern Virginia Daily*, the white students were having the time of their lives, the ones who wanted to attend classes did and the ones who didn't want to attend classes did not. The white students were being taught in private classes at the Union Hall, local churches or any vacant room in Front Royal large enough to house a class. They used Warren County High School teachers until Judge Paul ruled that they couldn't use the teachers to teach private schools as long as they were paid with public funds. Most of the teachers quit the public school system to go to work for the private education foundation. It appeared that the only effect the school closing had on the white students was the location of the classes.

God, I became like my Daddy, reading everything in sight. I would read the news articles two and three times. I was reading the October 11 issue of the *Northern Virginia Daily*, "Warren Opens $175,000 School Fund Drive Campaign Gets $1,000 Donation." That same day we got a letter of encouragement with $1. The disparity between opportunities for the white folks and the opportunities for the colored folks were clear. I could understand my Daddy and his teachings. Daddy understood our inability to fight the white system and win, he understood our lack of education and he even understood that we did not have the same disposable income as the white folks. At the Viscose, the largest employer within thirty miles of Front Royal, the average hourly wage of the colored employees was $1.65 while the average wage of the white employees was $2.44. I was beginning to understand the problem all too well. I couldn't see the pot of gold at the end of the rainbow or how we could rise above this condition, not on this day. I said, "God damn white folks got everything and all we got is one dollar and no damn classes." Momma grabbed the paper from me and tore it up, saying, "You are getting just like your Daddy." She came at me with her shoe. "Using God's name in vain," she said, "Where did you hear such language?" With each word she hit me with the shoe. She whipped me all over the house, up the stairs and down the stairs. I ran underneath the bed and she threw the shoe at me under the bed. I stayed under the bed until Daddy came home from work. Momma told Daddy that she was concerned, because I was repeating that vile language from the obscene calls. Daddy gave me a real whipping. After he whipped me, he sat me down and explained that this whipping was for using the LORD's name in vain. I would say "but Daddy, but Daddy," he wouldn't let me get a word in. I learned to control my tongue.

It came out in the newspaper that the Union had voted to increase Union dues by $1 per week, per member to help finance private schools. That evening Daddy came in and slung his paper on the table. Usually, he came in and whacked Momma on the butt with the newspaper. When Momma asked if he had to contribute to the private school fund he said, "over my dead body." Daddy went to his Union meetings as religiously as we went to church. Prior to us filing the case to go to WCHS, Daddy was

Shop Steward for the Colored Union Workers. He had a habit of keeping his Union meeting minutes and grievance papers under the seat in his car. If I wanted to know something and I didn't have to go far. There they were.

[September 24, 1958 ...

> Motion by Bro.Kendall seconded by Bro.McCauley for the Union Hall to be opened for the children of Warren County High School if they so desire to use it. Motion by Bro.King, seconded by Bro.Straitiff to table the above motion. MOTION CARRIED.
>
> Sister Ireson stated that the Union Hall should not be used to teach Warren County High School students because the colored members helped to pay for the hall.
>
> Brother McCraw stated that he didn't have anything against the colored but if this motion put on the floor tonight didn't pass he would see to it that one would pass next week.]

I had heard Daddy say, "If there is something they want to get accomplished, they will bring two three hundred of their buddies to vote their way and they can pass anything they want. There is so few of us Negroes we can't get anything through." I was concerned because if this was the way it was, I may not have a Daddy. I read on:

[October 1, 1958 ...

> Brother Clifton Kendall and Brother William McCauley would like to withdraw their motion that was tabled last week which read as follows:
>
> "Motion by Bro. Kendall seconded by Bro. McGauley for the Union Hall to be opened for the children of Warren County High School if they so desire to use it. Motion by Bro.King seconded by Bro. Slraitiff to table the above motion, MOTION CARRIED."
>
> Motion by Bro. Elwood Miller seconded by Brother Prillaman that the Business Agent to notify Mr. Duncan Gibb, the Chairman of the Fact Finding Committee, to establish private Schools—that they may use the Union Hall.
>
> Bro. Wade Byrd reported on the school problem in Warren County, he feels that we should raise union dues $1.00 per member to help Warren County Schools crisis.
>
> Motion by Bro.Wade Byrd seconded by Bro. Prillaman that we increase Union dues $1.00 per week per member to help finance private schools and this money to be turned over to Duncan Gibb and his committee to do with as they see fit, in order to maintain Private Schools and if there is

any individual or group that don't want to support this assessment that they go to the Union Hall and collect their money. Also if at any time this Body deems it practical they can cancel the increase by a vote of the Body of this Local. Brother Wade Byrd stated that he would like to see the engineer department to have one chairman to represent the white and the colored group.

Motion by Bro. Wade Byrd seconded by Bro. Howard King to have one chairman to represent the white and colored group in the engineer dept., if this isn't possible now, then it should come into effect this fall when officers are nominated for the various Departments. MOTION CARRIED.

Motion by Bro. Wade Byrd seconded by Bro. Allen Jenkins that in the future we nominate all members from the BODY to be sent to any convention and that no members be sent from any particular group. MOTION CARRIED.]

Well Daddy wouldn't be going to any more conventions. Let's see what's on the next page.

[October 15, 1958 ...

Brother Chas. Wines stated he would like to have a hand count vote instead of a secret ballot.

Motion by Bro. Wines, seconded by Bro. Rumsey Alger that we have a vote of hands instead of secret ballot on the motion. MOTION CARRIED.

Bro. Wade Byrd stated that he put his motion on the floor and thinks it's a good one and will appreciate all the support he can get for it.

Brothers E.K. White, Elwood Miller, Curly Cole, Ray Beaty, Ernie Prillaman and Tom Kerns rise in favor of this motion.

Brother Leadman stated that up until now I haven't taken a stand on this issue, but tonight I rise in favor of this motion, I would like to say a few things about the relationship that existed between the white and colored races before this issue was brought up. When this Union was organized the colored met in Free Town and we met up-town. After we built the Union Hall we allowed the colored members to meet with us. There was a motion from the floor for the colored kids to play Little League baseball. There is a possibility that the things the colored race have gained over the years that could be lost.

Bro. Muntzing stated he was probably fighting a losing battle, but I rise to say a few words on this motion. We have members from other counties who will not benefit from this one-dollar assessment, I think we should take this into consideration.

Bro. Julian Carper, stated I am rising as a Member of Local #371 ONLY. I am not representing the International of State AFL-CIO. The Governor of the State of Virginia has closed the school in Warren County, and other the Supreme Court has stated what the law is. I think we should abide by it. Therefore, I am against this motion.
Bro. Garfield Prather stated the Judges have ruled you can't use teachers to teach Private Schools as long as they are paid with Public Funds and there is a possibility they may rule it is illegal to take a dollar out of our pay to support Private Schools.]
Garfield Prather was the only colored member to speak.

[Bro. Leadman stated that Bro. Julian Carper and he have been friends for a long time, but I don't go along with his statement. I have met with the colored group several times concerning this problem, we asked them to withdraw, but not give up anything they have won in court, but, let us open the school and when the state and federal Governments settle their legal battle, they will get what they won in court.
Motion by Bro. Wade Byrd seconded by Bro. Prillaman that we increase Union dues $1.00 per week per member to help finance private schools and this money to be turned over to Duncan Gibb and his committee to do with as they see fit, in order to maintain private schools. If there is any individual or group that don't want to support this raise in Union dues that they go to the Union Hall and collect their money. Also, if at any time this Body deems it practical, they can cancel the increase by a vote of the body of this Local. Result of Voting is as follows: FOR 281 AGAINST 83.
Motion by Bro. Tom Kerns, Seconded by Bro. Clifton Kendall, any member desiring to have their dollar refunded, must give their name to Local Business Agent Mr. C. E. Leadman or the Office Secretary Mr. Wm. J. Farrell, and certify that they want their dollar refunded. This certification must be made on or before Saturday Noon, October 25, 1958, and also that this Notice be posted on this effect. MOTION CARRIED.
Motion by E. K. White, Seconded by Bro. Wade Byrd that a three-man committee be appointed by the President to disburse these funds, and that it be put in a separate account from the regular Union accounts, that the name of this committee be: Local #371, educational committee, that the treasurer be bonded and that two signatures of the three members appear on all checks issued. MOTION CARRIED. The President appointed to this committee: HOWARD KING-Treasurer, ELWOOD MILLER and THOMAS KERNS.

Bro. Herman Fitzgerald stated that it doesn't matter where you live this is a problem for all counties, I am sure if this would happen in some other county the people of Warren would come to their aid.]

[October 22, 1958 . . .

Bro. Leadman stated that someone called Mr. Hill in Richmond and notified him that we had passed a motion to increase Union dues $1.00 each week to help finance private schools in Warren County. The NAACP then notified American Viscose in Philadelphia that they would bring an injunction against them if they increased Union dues one dollar per member to finance private schools. Brother Lillard stated that last week one of the colored members ask? "Was the motion out of order?" One week has passed and to the best of my knowledge the motion was in order.

Motion by Bro. Wade Byrd, seconded by Bro. Elwood Miller that we recind the action taken last week pertaining to Union dues, and adopt the voluntary check-off system. MOTION CARRIED.

Motion by Bro. Elwood Miller, seconded by Bro. Robert Pullen, that we discontinue sponsoring the Heavenly Gospel Chorus program each week over W.F.T.R. MOTION CARRIED.]

The Heavenly Gospel course was a colored group that had a Gospel music program on the radio on Sunday morning. I remembered reading a letter in the paper from Rev. Baltimore stating that neither he nor any member of his group were involved in the integration movement. It was that old tactic of divide and conquer. The whole world was mad at Daddy. One more shouldn't make a difference, except Rev. Baltimore's wife was Momma's best friend. We didn't want to see them mad at each other. Daddy said, "One with courage and God on his side is a mighty army." I guess we just had to be that mighty army.

[Brother Leadman stated the colored people of this community have progressed very good over the last ten years. Some of them must have forgotten about this when they taken the action to enter Warren County High School after the county had started a modern school for them.

Bro. Wade Byrd stated that he didn't want to harm any of the colored people that didn't have anything to do with this integration. On the other hand, I don't think the small colored group that is responsible for this trouble has shown any consideration toward us.]

The Union ended up with a volunteer check-off system and took in an average of $1,600 to $1,700 weekly donation to the Warren County Educational Foundation to support private schools. A majority of the colored employees supported the private school for fear of harassment and losing their jobs. I guess we can say Daddy won because he didn't have to support private schools for white children while we were still out of school, however, Daddy was laid off.

On December 11, 1958, the twenty-two Negro students were enrolled into the integrated schools in Washington, D.C., under the sponsorship and funded by the Front Royal Educational Fund, a concerned citizens group from Washington, D.C., and the surrounding areas. The Co-Chairmen, Burma A. Whitted, and William B. Bryant; Treasurer, Frank Coleman; and Washington, D. C. committee members: Mrs. Emily Taft Douglas, Mrs. Herbert Marshall, Mrs. Agnes Meyer, Mrs. Irene Osborne, Mrs. James Scott, Mrs. Michael Shapiro and Mrs. John Steele. The committee had to pay $79 for tuition for each in Junior High School for the period covering the remainder of the semester and $88 for tuition for each student in Senior High School for the balance of the first semester, plus transportation, room and board for the children to be housed in Washington, D.C.

My brothers Jimmy and Bubble, Rebecca Fletcher, Steve Travis and I stayed with Rev. Carter, his wife and daughter. Rev. Carter was the pastor at Mt. Nebo Baptist Church in Happy Creek. He commuted from Washington D.C. every first and third Sunday to preach at Mt. Nebo. The committee paid Rev. Carter $7.00 weekly for room and board for all five of us.

Rebecca and I slept in the same bed. My sister and I had to share the same bed. I hated sleeping with my sister. We had a string tied from the headboard to the footboard that divided the bed in half. I made up my side of the bed using separate sheets and blankets and my sister did likewise. There was no way that I could separate this bed without making Rebecca feel uncomfortable. I slept on the very edge of the bed.

Rebecca was in the tenth grade, she was older than me and she went to high school while I went to junior high. She was use to being away from home because before all this, she went to school in Manassas. In the early days of being away from home, I cried myself to sleep most nights. I didn't know anyone in my school. I didn't dress grown-up like the other kids. The kids made fun of me. I was behind in most of my classes and didn't know the answers, and that made me feel dumb.

Rev. Carter's daughter, Delores was one of the sweetest people in Washington, D.C. She was twenty-eight years old and she had a good government job. In the evening, I would talk to Delores and cry because the other kids made fun of me. She said, "Oh, I have a lot of experience with being made fun of, look at me, I'm fat and the other kids had a lot of fun with me." I asked, "What did you do?" She said, "I learned to like myself and I learned to focus on the good side of me." She said, "I've been to Happy Creek and the country is beautiful." She told me to hold my head up and say with pride, "Yes, some people may think that where I come from is in the sticks and that people who live in the sticks are hicks. You should come with me sometime. We have grass, trees and lakes; some of the most beautiful country you will ever see." She took me shopping and bought me some grown-up clothes. I even began to fit in especially after my classmates saw me on TV and the teacher began to refer to me as a history maker. I don't know what I would have done without Delores.

We had been in school just about a week when Daddy got the following letter from Mrs. Marx.

[December 18, 1958
Dear Mr. Kilby:

Our committee met Tuesday evening to discuss fund raising and other matters. Mrs. Whitted and I think the parents should know where we stand financially.

At present the fund is "broke." We have paid out for tuition and help on board $1831.50. We have taken in only $714.00. We would not have been able to pay the tuition cost had not Mr. Coleman and I each loaned the fund $1,000.

About $3400 will be needed to pay tuition on February 1. Until we actually have enough funds to meet the tuition cost and pay back the $2,000 in loans, I don't think we should attempt to help more families pay board.

Several parents, in addition to Mrs. Coleman and Mrs. Rhodes, whom the committee promised to assist on board are saying they too need help. Perhaps you can get some contributions in Warren County to help these people and set-up a committee to handle it.

Unless contributions come in more generously than our expectations, the committee will have to restrict itself to tuition payments and paying for transportation to and from school and school lunches for those pupils who need it.

During the vacation Mrs. Whitted, another committee member and I hope to come to Front Royal to meet with the parents and discuss things. We would probably come Saturday, January 3. We think that the parents and children should agree on some ground rules for the children. A few seem to be spending too much time on dates and gossiping on the telephone. They are in Washington to get an education and have a lot of catching up to do.]

Thus, the Front Royal Educational Fund was established. The chairman of the Front Royal Committee was Delores Mansfield but she was not alone; Co-Chairmen in Front Royal and Warren County were: Bessie Pines, Annie Rhodes, Henrietta Baltimore and Katherine Butler. The funds were raised from private donations, church offerings and organization donations. Each week, the colored employees at American Viscose (Avtex) gave .25, .50, $1.00, $2.00, because this was all they could afford. The local churches held the collection plate for our cause. We (the twenty-two children) were required to make public appearances on TV talk shows, at the churches and other organizations. The committee from Washington met with us children every-other weekend from the time we entered the school system in D.C. until about June of 1962. The work of the Front Royal Educational committee did not stop when we were finally enrolled in Warren County High School. In fact, the most important role of the committee was assisting the students in understanding the seriousness of the role they were playing in a worldwide history-making drama, and assisting the children in adjusting to the everyday pressures of integration. They made sure that we walked and talked proper at the fund raising events, tutored us if we were having problems in any of our classes, counseled us through the emotional issues associated with going to school under such tremendous pressure and to simply to get us through school.

On February 10, 1959, U.S. Judge John Paul, ordered the re-opening of Warren County High School on a desegregated basis on Wednesday, February 18, 1959. The Warren County School Board attorney William J. Phillips, made a request for a delay to Chief Judge Simon E. Sabloff of the Fourth Circuit Court in Baltimore. Governor J. Lindsay Almond Jr. who fought integration to the end of the legal line before accepting some degree of it as inevitable, said he was displeased and hurt that any integration had to take place, but added: "The fact that no violence has occurred reflects the honor and good name of Virginia and the Nation continues to look on the state as a preserve of law and order." At the hearing in Judge Sabeloff's chambers, school board attorney William J. Phillips pleaded for the court's permission to keep the school closed until September. "We're defeated on integration, we realize that, but our stand now, sir, is that it is the feeling of the school board and the people of Warren County that the children, having been once upset this year, should not be subjected to the disservice of transferring them back, to the high school." He said the school board would pay the tuition for the twenty-two Negro applicants in the D.C. schools, where they have been attending." At another point, Phillips said, "I will be frank to tell the court that twenty-two Negroes will show up on Wednesday and maybe five or six whites. The school board has fourteen or fifteen teachers left out of the high school's staff of forty." Sabeloff said that he had sympathy for the school board's problem but, "I am going to say that the spectacle of empty school buildings and unoccupied teachers ought to be terminated. The refusal to reopen the school would violate the January 19, ruling of the State Supreme Court of appeals which called Virginia's Massive Resistance laws, including the school closing law unconstitutional. If you have a comprehensive deseg-regation plan, but it is fairly obvious you don't, the longer this continues, the more demoralized teachers will be, the more injury to pupils both white and Negro, and the more difficult it will be to comply with court orders."

We had almost forgot that we were soldiers in the midst of war. During dinner the night of February 10, Rev. Carter informed us of the judge's decision and he said that Friday would be our last day in school. Rebecca's father was coming to pick us up Saturday morning, therefore we had to have our belongings together. I emphatically announced that I could not go because Delores and I had plans to ride the subway. Delores quickly grabbed my hand and began patting it gently and explained that summer was coming and that I could come back to visit during the summer and we could ride the subway all over D.C. I quickly regained my composure and slipped into the soldier mode.

On our way home, Mr. Fletcher got lost in D.C. Bubble realized that we had gone around Dupont Circle four times. He asked, "Mr. Fletcher, have we been around this circle before, are we lost?" Mr. Fletcher pulled over and parked. He said, "I thought this circle looked familiar." He went over and talked to a taxi driver who led us out of D.C. During the briefing meeting, we shared our story of being lost in D.C. with the other children. We got a good laugh at Mr. Fletcher's expense saying to each other "Have we been around this circle before?"

The decision was made, the date was set and Mr. Hill was confident that there would be no more delays. The threats had increased to an all time high. Momma barred us kids from answering the phone. The tension was high and we were scared. The boys started milking the cows early because we had a meeting the night of February 17,1959 with the committee to make arrangements to get to the school. We had just finished dinner. I was at the kitchen sink washing dishes when I saw what seemed to be lightening go past the window but the loud blast told me that it was not lightening. Momma screamed and Daddy called out, "gun fire hit the floor!" This was the first time we were on the lower level of the house when gun-shots were fired at the house. The last thing that I remembered was the dog gave a howl as he took off across the field, doghouse and all. Daddy found him the next day trapped in the fence still chained to the doghouse. Evidently, I passed out, I woke to Momma slapping my face. She was scream-ing and crying hysterically because she thought that I was shot. We composed ourselves and left the house to go to the meeting. Momma said, "We will finish the dishes in the morning."

During the meeting, Daddy told the group what happened. He tried to maintain his composure. His voice was almost animated as he said, "I know what I have to do, we have come too far to give in to threats and intimidation; I am trusting and believing in Jesus. Just when Daddy's voice was about to give way, Rev. Frank started to pray, "Come by here Lord, come by here, your children need you Lord, come by here." We all got hung up in the praying and singing we almost forgot the war. Finally, Rev. Frank said that we needed to prepare for the next day. We talked about pick up times and who was riding with whom and we got our usual lecture on how we were supposed to act. Daddy, Mr. Dean and Mr. Fletcher couldn't get off from work. After we took care of the business, Rev. Frank prayed again and we left the church singing "Ain't gonna let nobody turn me around."

As I was getting ready for school I told myself that I wasn't scared. Then I told Momma that I was sick at the stomach. She said, "You just have butterflies in your stomach and as soon as you give those butterflies some of these pancakes they would settle down." With every bite, I thought my stomach was going to throw those pancakes back up into my face. I finally got ready and Mrs. Kathryn Butler came to pick us up. Momma kissed us and told the boys, "You stay close to your sister, you hear me." I could hear the fear in Momma's voice. When we got out of Mrs. Butler's car we had to walk past the crowd. I saw the policeman. Jimmy pushed me to keep me moving in front of him. As I walked past this big fat white woman, she yelled, we gonna kill all you little Niggers. I was so scared I urinated on myself. I just knew that I was going to die so I began to recite the 23rd Psalm to myself, I started, The Lord is my Shepard . . . yea though I walk through the valley of the shadow of death, I will fear no evil and somehow it was like I had summoned God and I wasn't afraid any more. Someone began to sing, "We Shall Overcome." I couldn't carry a tune but singing always encouraged me.

As Warren County opened its doors on a desegregated basis, only the twenty-three students involved in *Betty Kilby et. al. vs. Warren County School Board* showed-up for registration. The history makers were: James Kilby, 11th grade; John Kilby, 10th grade; Betty Kilby, 8th grade; Elizabeth Dean, 12th grade; Suetta Dean, 9th grade; Louise Dean, 8th grade; Marybelle Coleman, 8th grade; Delores Coleman, 9th grade; Faye Coleman, 11th grade; Gwendolyn Baltimore, 11th grade; Archie Pines, 11th grade; Matthew Pines Jr., 8th grade; Rebecca Fletcher, 10th grade; Joyce Henderson, 11th grade; Steven Travis, 10th grade; Frank Grier 11th grade; John R. Jackson Jr., 9th grade; Barbara Jackson, 8th grade; Charles Lewis, 10th grade; Geraldine Rhodes, 10th grade; Dorothy Rhodes, 9th grade; Ann Rhodes, 12th grade. Joyce Henderson changed her mind about Warren County High School and went back to the school she was attending. Elizabeth Dean, a senior also, changed her mind about Warren County High School. She wanted to complete the requirements for a certificate in Cosmetology at the school she was attending in Washington, D.C., leaving Ann Rhodes as the only senior.

Each side stood steadfast in the support of their stand on integration or segregation. Charles E. Leadman, Business Agent for Local 371, Textile Workers Union of America, together in a mass meeting led over 1,000 white parents of former Warren County High School students, and contributors to the Warren County Education Foundation. Unbelievable! This was the union, the very same union that my father said was supposed to protect the rights of all its members, the same union that my Daddy was once a Shop Stewart for the colored union workers. The purpose of this meeting was to settle the issue of whether to send their high school children to WCHS or choose their own methods of educating their children. Hugh D. McCormick, a Front Royal attorney introduced the following resolution that was approved without a single dissenting vote.

[WHEREAS, we the citizens of Front Royal and Warren County, feel grateful to the Warren County Educational Foundation for outstanding services rendered our community in establishing and maintaining an efficient school for our children during this period of emergency, and

WHEREAS, we are indebted to the teachers for their understanding and help in the education of our children, and

WHEREAS, it is our opinion that it will be in the best interest of all children of Warren County to continue their studies without interruption for the remainder of this school year,

NOW THEREFORE BE IT RESOLVED, that we the citizens of Front Royal and Warren County request the Warren County Educational Foundation to continue the operation of the Foundation School for the remainder of this school year and that the teachers remain with the Foundation during this period.]

Not a single white student showed up to register or to attend classes during the 1958-1959 school term.

Many, many years after February 18, 1958, Daddy talked about the day that we entered Warren County High School. Daddy admitted that he was as scared as all of us children, but he couldn't show his fear. He said that someone threw a hammer at him. He said it came so close he could feel the air as it flew past his head. He said that his heart stopped for a moment and he stood paralyzed. He told us that he was ordered to report to the main office. Like so many times before he went to take the elevator up to the first floor. He said that when the elevator opened, all he could see was the empty shaft. Had he stepped into the elevator, he would surely have died by falling down the elevator shaft. Someone had removed the "Do Not Use" sign from the elevator. When he finally got to the office, he was informed that the kids were all right.

After the first day, school was pretty exciting. The number of students dwindled down to eighteen. We had fourteen teachers and a principal (James Duff) who held us in such low esteem that you couldn't even get him to say a mere "Good morning." Some classes had as few as one student with a maximum of five students per class. Most of the teachers were civil. They were no more accustomed to teaching Negroes, as we were accustomed to learning from white teachers. The three-story building was beautiful and huge. The building was so large that we would cut across the auditorium to get from one side of the building to the other. I felt safer in this building than I felt at home with the gunshots constantly being fired at the house, crosses burned in the yard, bloody sheet on the mailbox, the farm animals mutilated and the constant threatening phone calls.

This was a difficult time for Ann Rhodes because she did not have a prom and she was deprived of her graduation ceremony. We received half credit for each class for the period covering February 18 to the end of the school term. Most of us attended summer school including the only senior, Ann. When Ann completed summer school in August, she became the single public high school graduate in Warren County for the 1958-1959 school year. The school board refused to give Ann her diploma even though she had sufficient credits. Twenty years later, she received a call from the school board office asking her to stop by the office and pick up her diploma.

The Atlantic City, New Jersey Chapter of the Improved Benevolent Protective Order of Elks of the World honored Ann Rhodes with graduation festivities. Since the Education Foundation had money that was earmarked for the second semester of our education in Washington, D.C., and wasn't used because WCHS re-opened, they sponsored a trip for the eighteen students to go to Atlantic City from August 22-28, 1959 to celebrate Ann's graduation. The committee bought a soft pink material with blue embroidered flowers and commissioned Mrs. Pearl Jordan to make dresses for the girls so that we could be easily identified at Ann's prom party. The boys were asked to wear dark suits and light blue shirts.

Besides going to school in D.C., most of us had not traveled beyond the boundaries of Virginia. We were happy to be celebrating Ann's graduation, prom and all the things high school graduates do that we couldn't do in Warren County. My only bus experience was the tattered and torn school bus. The chartered bus that we rode to Atlantic City was a palace when compared to the school bus.

We stayed in the homes of the Elks members. I stayed with the Johnson family. They had a daughter a couple of years younger than me. These people didn't work all the time like us farmers. Their daughter took ballet and piano lessons. When they asked what I did for fun, I told them about going to town on Saturday morning and getting twenty-five cents to buy candy. They had a dish on the coffee table filled with candy. They pointed to the dish and told me to eat as much candy as I wanted. As I reached for the candy, I imagined Daddy watching me and I only took one piece of candy. They wanted to know what it was like growing up on the farm. I told them about my Daddy getting up at 4 AM to milk the cows before going to work at the Viscose and how we planted the garden and harvested fruits and vegetables. Mrs. Johnson said, "You really don't have any time to play and have fun." She said, "Well young lady, all you are going to do this weekend is play, eat lots of candy and have fun." I followed those orders. She asked, "Do you dance?" I told her, "My brother Bubble says I dance like a polka." She put on the music and I jumped around like popcorn popping and Mrs. Johnson kept saying, "Slow down, feel the music, move to the beat of the music, close your eyes and feel the beat."

We went down on the Boardwalk. It was the first time that I saw the ocean. The waves were so soothing. It was like heaven. That Saturday night was the prom party. I tried the new dance steps. I closed my eyes and I kept bumping into people. Bubble told me to sit down because I was embarrassing him and making a fool of myself. Since Mrs. Whitted was in charge and she didn't tell me to sit down, I continued to have fun. Because of our outfits, everyone knew who we were and they would tell us how brave and courageous we were. It was a very special weekend, lots of love, praise and fun. When I got ready to leave, the Johnsons fixed me a care package with all of my favorite goodies. I had so many goodies; it was enough for the whole family to share. The ride home was very quiet; we were all tired and sleepy.

The summer vacation ended and it was time to put on our armor and become little soldiers. The white kids enrolled in Warren County High School. The peace and tranquility ended. Our safe environment was no longer safe. Our class size increased to fifteen to twenty. The Negroes were all spread out. Even though there were four eighth graders, I was the only Negro in most of my classes. I was in a lower homeroom class because of the half-credit deal until I reached the tenth grade. I was assigned to Mr. Leckie's eighth-grade homeroom. Every morning I walked across the room to take my seat in the first seat in the first row next to the window. As I walked across the room I would walk straight and tall, put on my happy face and say "Good Morning." Mr. Leckie was the only person to respond.

Some of my classmates stared, others made ugly faces and some were downright mean and nasty. When I encountered the mean and nasty ones, I would say to myself, "I am a child of God full of grace and beauty, with God on my side, I have nothing to fear." In the more critical times, I would make a fist and pretend that God was holding my hand. The feeling of God holding my hand made me smile. One day, as most days, someone called me a Nigger, this white girl saw me clinch my fist, smile and walk away. Her curiosity got the best of her and she wanted to know how I could take the constant harassment and smile. I looked her straight in the eye and said, "Because I am a child of God full of grace and beauty." She looked right back at me and said, "you are crazy" and she walked away.

We continued to ride separate school buses. After school a bus picked up the Negro children at Warren County High School, drove us to Criser Combined Colored School where we would transfer to busses that transported colored children home. The bus ride from Warren County High School to Criser Combined Colored School gave us an opportunity to discuss what went on during the day at school.

From the very first day, we knew that it was not safe to walk the halls alone, take the short cut through the auditorium from one side of the building to the other side of the building or even go to the restroom alone. During our first weekend meeting with the committee, the main topic of discussion was safety issues. When we had the building all to ourselves, we became very comfortable in the building. We were told not to trust anyone except each other. We studied each other's schedules to team-up as much as possible to protect each other. We shared information about students and teachers who could not be trusted.

Geraldine Rhodes and I tried out for majorettes but neither one of us made the squad. I had no experience whatsoever but Geraldine was good. The committee didn't encourage us. They simply said, "It would have been nice, but you are there to get an education." Rev. Frank said, "You are pioneers, your reward will come from a good education." Bubble and Charles Lewis tried out for basketball. Charles was such an outstanding and impressive player; he made the team. He was told that if he were on the team there would be no one to play. Charles agonized over the decision to stay on the team and keep the school from having a team or give up his dream. Charles gave up his basketball dream for a quality education.

Faye Coleman was the only senior during the 1959–60 school year among the twenty-one heroes. During the Christmas holidays, Faye got engaged and she decided to get married right away. The committee tried to talk Faye out of quitting school, but Faye couldn't take it any longer, and besides she had to go to summer school to graduate because of the half-credit deal.

Each year the enrollment of the white students at WCHS increased more and more and the number of Negro students hovered between sixteen and nineteen. As the number of white students increased, so did the tension and harassment of the Negro students. During the 1960-61 school term, the school board allowed private organizations to formulate. The senior class formulated an organization to sponsor the senior prom. My brother James and Frank Grier were the only two seniors. They were not allowed to join the organization nor were they allowed to attend the prom. Again the committee took the position that we were at WCHS to get an education. Besides, there were larger issues. Our mothers couldn't get jobs cleaning houses in Front Royal or Warren County. They had to get up at 4 AM and ride sixty miles to the Northern Virginia area for work. Our NAACP lawyers were fighting with the local Union because our fathers who worked at the Viscose were under attack and risked losing their jobs. Our farm animals were being mutilated and poisoned. Someone had come onto our property, took a very thin wire and wrapped it around all four ankles of one of our calves. As the calf grew the wire cut into the calf's ankles cutting off the circulation causing the calf's hooves to rot off. As Daddy had the calf put to sleep, Daddy prayed for the person. It was hard to think of someone who would torture a poor dumb animal as a person. Everyone including the committee was growing tired and weary.

Since James and Frank would be the first of the twenty-one heroes to officially graduate from an integrated class, the committee would sponsor a celebration at the Lodge. It was a long and trying school year and at last, we celebrated Jimmy and Frank's graduation. It was not as nice or elaborate as Ann's celebration.

The day after the graduation, my ten-year old brother Gene was playing in the yard when two white boys riding their bikes stopped in the front of our house. They thought Gene was alone; they called him racial names and came after him. Gene came running in the house and told us about the incident. Clarence Williams, one of Bubble's friends from the loop was visiting. We all went outside and sat on the front porch. Later that day, the boys came back down the road and they stopped again. Jimmy and Bubbled dared them to come over into our yard and pick on somebody their size. When they came into the yard Gene started to throw mud pies at them, they ran, got on their bicycles and left.

Later that evening the police knocked on the door and asked for "James Kilby." Daddy said, "I'm James Kilby, what do you want?" They said, "We want your boy." Daddy asked to see his warrant. When Daddy looked at the warrant, he said. "Your warrant says that you want adult James Kilby, that must be me." Daddy was up in the officer's face saying, "You want James Kilby, that's me, take me." The officer got frustrated and took Daddy down to the police station. As Daddy was leaving with the officer, he instructed Momma to call Rev. Frank. We told Momma what happened with the boys. Just as Rev. Frank was pulling into the yard, Daddy and the Police officer pulled in too. The officer arrested Jimmy. When the Officer cuffed Jimmy and attempted to put him in the police vehicle Daddy jumped in too, saying "If you are arresting my son I'm going too." Rev. Frank said, "Arrest me too." They all went off with the officer. Jimmy was booked for disorderly conduct. Frank Grier was also arrested and booked. Both boys posted bond and were allowed to go home. During the trial, they both pled innocent. Frank Grier was acquitted. Jimmy was convicted of disorderly conduct, was fined $50 and given a thirty-six day suspended sentence and a bench warrant was issued for Bubble charging him with the same offense.

The lawyers informed Daddy that it was just a matter of time before Jimmy would be subpoenaed to testify against Bubble. Daddy told Jimmy to go down in the field and stay there until he sent for him. Momma packed Jimmy's bag and Jimmy was hauled off to D.C. When the police officers came to serve the papers on Jimmy, Daddy told them that he didn't know where Jimmy was nor did he know when he would be home. Daddy said, "He's a man now, he's on his own." The police officers watched the house for days. We got some peace from the Night Riders because of the police presence.

During Bubble's hearing, Daddy was cited for contempt of court for his failure to cooperate with the Warren County Juvenile Court. Bubble's case was continued several times because of the Commonwealth's inability to summons Jimmy as a witness against Bubble. At Daddy's contempt hearing Judge J. Adair Moore admonished Daddy for his lack of cooperation in assisting the law enforcement officers in serving Jimmy with a summons. Daddy noted an appeal and posted a $250 bond for his appearance in court on September 3, 1961. At Daddy's appeal hearing, Charles F. Yates, a guard at American Viscose Corporation, testified that, "Kilby refused to accept the summons for his own appearance in court until he had a clarification on company policy about accepting service of legal papers. Upon being advised of company policy to cooperate with law enforcement officers. Kilby accepted service but refused to be interviewed." Judge Moore testified that "he admonished Kilby on June 28 to cooperate with officers after Kilby told the court his son had been at home when an officer called with the summons. He told the officer that his son was away. Judge Moore recalled that Kilby told the court he denied his son was home because he did not feel he had to discuss his personal business with the officer." He further testified that, "On July 12, the day the contempt fine was levied, Kilby admitted that he had talked to his son by telephone and had not told him of the summons."

Judge Elliott Marshall ruled, that the court did not have the authority to order Daddy to cooperate with or assist law enforcement in the service of a summons. He prefaced his remarks with the following statement, "The court has a right to the respect of every person who enters the courtroom, good citizenship requires that officers be assisted in the performance of their duties. However, the law does not require people to be good citizens." Daddy was acquitted of the contempt charges. Bubble's case was continued indefinitely, pending the summoning of a Commonwealth's witness.

The school authorities refused to accept Bubble into WCHS until the final disposition of his case. Our NAACP lawyers had to go back to Federal Judge Paul in Harrisonburg. Judge Paul issued an order restraining the School board from refusing to let Bubble attend classes. Jimmy evaded being summoned to testify against Bubble by staying out of Warren County. Bubble was never prosecuted for the crime.

At my twenty-five year reunion, Kenneth Hamilton apologized. He said, "When I was young and foolish I said and did some foolish things to you and your family and I am truly sorry for all the ugly things that I did." He was one of the boys who was involved in the rock-throwing incident. Kenneth and his friend Tony Spencer threw spitballs at me for a solid year in Mrs. Czarniski's class until one day when I blurted out, "Mrs. Czarniski, will you please make Tony and Kenneth stop throwing spitballs at me?" We all got detention. Tony and Kenneth for throwing spitballs and I got detention for being disruptive in class.

During the 1961–62 school term the infant plaintiffs who were juniors and seniors were offered an opportunity to go to Winchester, Virginia, to Douglass High School to take a test and the test scores were sent to the

United Negro College Fund and various colleges. Evidently, Bubble received high scores because he was awarded a $500 scholarship and was accepted to Fisk University. Bubble was incredibly smart. He rarely studied, rarely brought a book home and usually had the best report card. One of Bubble's high school teachers, Mrs. McFall, told Momma and Daddy, that "there was no telling what Bubble could do if he applied himself." Very few white teachers gave us our due. If we got a "B" on our report card, more often than not, we probably deserved an "A." In the fall, Bubble was the first in our family to go off to college. He was incredible; he grew up on the farm where play was a rarity. He dreamed of participating in sports, never played on any teams, didn't play much for fun, went to college and made the football team.

Momma had become quite enterprising. She had to go to work down in the country. She worked, bought what we needed using the same economically thrift habits that she had practiced growing-up and she saved enough money to buy a car. She decided to buy a station wagon even though she didn't drive. She hired a driver and transported workers from Front Royal to Falls Church six days a week. The market for transportation was so good she added another station wagon and a second driver.

During that summer Daddy and the NAACP negotiated with local businesses to hire colored employees in public positions. The NAACP also organized a campaign to eat at the local restaurants. We had about six to eight groups that visited various restaurants to attempt to be served lunch, dinner or a snack. I was in Mrs. Juanita Barbour's group. We went to the Belle Boyd Restaurant. We were stopped at the door. Rev. Frank's group went to the Royal Dairy. They ordered and were served ice cream sundaes. The white folks harassed the owner of the Royal Dairy so bad he had a heart attack. Daddy had a group of boys including Bubble. According to Bubble, they went to the first restaurant and they were met at the door and turned away. The restaurant owner had called the police. Daddy went home changed vehicles and went to another restaurant, again they were refused service. The police told Daddy, "Take these boys and go home." Daddy told the officer, "All we are trying to do is get something to eat." Daddy went home changed vehicles and went back to the first restaurant. The police said, "Kilby, how many damn cars do you have? You go home now and take these boys, if I catch you out here again, I'm gonna have to lock you up." We all met back at our house, talked about the project and had a cookout on our new grill.

By the 1962–63 school term, there was only four of the original twenty-one left, Steven Travis, Matthew Pines, Barbara Jackson and me. Steven was a year late graduating because he was out for an extended sick period in 1960. Matthew was the last to graduate because of the half-credit deal, all of the infant plaintiffs who were in the eighth grade had to go to summer school every summer to graduate on schedule. Barbara and I went to summer school every summer since 1959 in order to graduate on schedule in June 1963.

Since there were so few of us left it was hard to maintain our buddy system. For the first time since 1958, I didn't have one of my brothers in school to watch over me. Over the course of the years during integration, I had developed a spirit of independence and confidence. If I couldn't find a buddy to walk across the auditorium then I would walk across the auditorium alone. I knew better, but I did it anyway. Another rule that we had was never to live by a pattern. I had established a pattern. The committee rarely met with the infant plaintiffs, Rev. Frank moved and we were left without counsel. There were not the constant reminders of safety. Even the Night Riders had diminished to a rare occurrence. There was a false sense of safety and security.

One day as I was crossing the auditorium alone, there were three boys hiding behind the stage. I was grabbed from behind, blindfolded, mouth taped and raped. They raped me for the thrill of violating a Nigger. One of the boys didn't have a rubber and the other boys told him that his penis would rot off if he stuck it in me without a rubber. He was charged with holding my arms and hands down. When the first boy climbed on top of me, he pushed himself in me so hard and aggressively that I thought he was going to tear my insides out. He moaned and groaned like the hogs in the barnyard. I saw myself watching the violation thinking it was my grandmother laying on the floor with old man Dick Finks laying on top of her. When the second boy climbed on top of me he was quiet and expressionless. I thought about my dog when she was stuck with the neighbor's dog. I tried to beat that dog to death when Bubble held me back explaining that the dog was inside my dog and his penis swelled up inside my dog and they couldn't be detached until the swelling went down. I passed out hoping that I would die from this experience.

I woke up alone on the stage floor behind the curtain exposed and violated. I got up, removed the tape from my mouth and went to the girl's restroom. I pulled a handful of paper towels, ran cold water on them and retreated to one of the stalls. I heard the bell ring signaling the end of the class period. I put my feet up against the door so that no one would know that I was in the stall. I sat quietly as tears rolled down my cheeks. Then I heard the bell ring again signaling the start of the next class period. Like a zombie, I cleaned myself up, walked back across the auditorium to avoid going past the principal's office. I went to my locker, got my coat and left the school by way of the lower backside door. I walked to J. J. Newberry's five and dime store. I walked straight to the girdle section, took a girdle off the shelf, went in the dressing room, put on the girdle and walked to Rev. Frank's house. When I got to Rev. Frank's house, I remembered that he had moved to Philadelphia during the summer. I walked to the colored section of town. I saw Carroll Freedman, a high school dropout and Bubble's friend. He asked, "Are you all right?" I said, "No, I'm sick. Can you take me home?" He said, "Yes." I got in his car and he drove me home. He said, "You don't look so good, do you want me to take you to the doctor or call someone?" I cried so loud and hard he drove me home without uttering another word.

I cooked dinner, cleaned the kitchen and went to my room. I sat in my closet behind the clothes trying to figure out what to do. I had concluded that I wanted to die but I couldn't go to heaven if I committed suicide. I wanted the hell on earth to be over, I couldn't die and the hell would continue. I had no one to talk to. If I told Barbara, she would be scared too, besides she would feel sorry for me. She may think it was my fault. I knew it wasn't safe walking across the stage alone. Momma would say, "You are so determined." I tried to imagine what Rev. Frank would say. I tried all the techniques that Rev. Frank taught me to survive a crisis. My Daddy couldn't protect me. He couldn't protect our livestock. He couldn't even protect our dog. The pain wouldn't stop. It wasn't a physical pain. The boys didn't hurt my body, they broke my spirit and I couldn't get it back. I had no will to live.

A couple of weeks later, Carroll came by the house while we were waiting for the bus to see if I was all right. I told him that I was driving to school. He said, "I bet I can beat you to the cemetery." I said, "Oh, you want to die too." The way he looked at me, immediately I realized he was talking about the cemetery as the ending point of the race. I said, "Sure." I made Gene and Pat ride the school bus. As I got in the car Gene yelled, "I'm gonna tell." I yelled back, "I don't care." Carroll offered to let me get in the front since I was a girl. I refused the advantage saying that we could start side-by-side on Happy Creek Road and that he could have the right lane. He said, "Damn girl, you crazy." As we lined-up on Happy Creek Road with me in the wrong lane, I prayed that God would take me quickly. I said my prayers. "Yea though I walk through the valley of the shadow of death, I will fear no evil" took on a new meaning this day. We counted down one, two, three. I was in the lead before we got to "dead man's curve." As I rounded dead man's curve, I yelled, "God take me home." I took the curve without fear or flinching, it was the most thrilling sensation that I had ever felt. God didn't take me home. Instead he gave me the thrill of my life, let me beat the King of Happy Creek Road and brought a smile back to my very sad face. In the following days and weeks, I raced all the time. I became Queen of Happy Creek Road.

One day as I was racing, there was some chickens in the road as I approached dead man's curve. I plowed through the chickens yelling "fried chicken tonight." To my surprise, the next day there was the wounded chicken in a cage for me to see every time I passed. Finally, I couldn't take it any more. One evening on the way home, I stopped at the house hoping that the people who lived in the house were evil white people and they would throw me in the well. The well would be my final resting place and my death would be swift. I was prepared to meet my maker. I knocked on the door. When the woman came to the door, without saying hello, I cried out, "I'm the one, I'm the one who hit your chicken. I'm sorry." She asked, "Are you one of them kids racing out this road?" I said, "Yes, ma'am." She said, "You know one of you kids gonna get killed on that curve" pointing to dead man's curve. I said, "Yes ma'am." She asked, "Are you sorry enough to give up that racing?" I said, "Yes ma'am." The whole time I am crying uncontrollably. She said, "Come here child, I think you need a hug." I held on to that woman as if she was my last friend in this world. The next time the boys came to race, I said, "No, I am quitting racing, there is no challenge to beating you little country boys." I had insulted the guys and they didn't come around anymore. I didn't race again. Destroying my life was one thing and I had no right to destroy someone else's property.

I couldn't eat and I couldn't sleep. I was explosive. One day at the beginning of the class before the teacher came into the class, a girl by the name of Donna Kersey balled up a sheet of notebook paper, threw it at me and hit me up side the head. I picked up the paper, walked over to her put one hand around her neck and with the other hand stuffed the paper in her mouth. As I was holding her neck, I heard Rev. Frank's voice saying, "For every action, there is a consequence, ask yourself, what is the consequence and are you willing to pay the price?" I let go of her neck and walked back to my desk. The room was quiet and no one said a word. I was in trouble and I didn't know how to heal myself.

I got to the point where I could yield my will, my body would go limp and I would pass out. I was hospitalized for a week. While I was in the hospital, Rev. Pendleton came by to visit. He was an orderly in the hospital but I knew him from church. He knew the family and was a distant relative. He sat on the foot of my bed and he asked, "What's wrong with you child?" As tears rolled down my cheeks, I said, "I want to die." He asked, "Why?" I said, "Because I'm tired of living." He said in a half joking manner, "me too." I looked at him kind of puzzled, he said, "The hardest part of the journey is at the very end when the race is almost won." He asked, "How long have you been in Warren County High School?" I said, "Four years, I graduate in June." He said, "This old race is almost over, the best part of your life is just around the corner, God has given you a job, He will give you strength to make it through. It was a big job for such a little girl like you but you can do it. Just keep your hand in God's hand." I was never quite the same but I survived.

I finally graduated. I wasn't allowed to attend my high school prom. On my graduation night the zipper on my dress broke and I was the last person to leave the school. As my classmates hugged and kissed, there were no hugs for me. I hugged myself and looked toward heaven and whispered, "thank you." I sat on the table waiting for my parents to bring me another dress so that I could leave that rented cap and gown.

All my friends from the surrounding schools came to my graduation party. Most of the committee members came to bring closure to our struggle for a quality education. This was the last party for the infant plaintiffs involved in *Betty Ann Kilby vs. Warren County School Board.*

Chapter 4

Clouds of Joy

*I had no education beyond high school; no job skills
and I couldn't even balance the checkbook, but
every dark cloud brought joy to my life.*

After my high school graduation, my friend Alease and I decided to move to Washington, D.C. and get a job. Alease had an aunt (Ms. Conti) that lived in D.C. Ms. Conti was a professional woman. She worked for the government. She said we could live with her for free until we got on our feet. We packed our bags and Alease's father drove us to DC. We didn't have any money or any job searching skills. Ms. Conti, being a career woman didn't have any food in her refrigerator. We were like two fish out of water. It was my first taste of being out in the world without someone watching over me directing my every decision. We hadn't been out looking for a job because we didn't know where to go or how to get around on the bus. We hadn't eaten anything except the junk food that Alease brought from home since we arrived in D.C. a little over twenty-four hours ago. We couldn't leave the house because we were afraid of the city life and we didn't have a key to get back in the house.

Within two days, Daddy sent my brother Jimmy over to Ms. Conti's to check out our living situation. When Jimmy arrived, Ms. Conti wasn't home and neither Alease nor I knew what time she was coming home. Jimmy took us to dinner at the Florida Avenue Grill. It was just like Daddy had explained; a black restaurant, black owned and operated and we could sat down and eat. Wow! Alease and I tried to play it off like we weren't hungry but we scarfed down the food and it was clearly evident that we hadn't eaten in twenty-four hours. When we arrived back to Ms. Conti's after dinner, Jimmy went in the house and looked in the refrigerator and the cabinets. Alease told Jimmy that Ms. Conti was going grocery shopping and that she would be bringing food home that night. Jimmy left the newspaper with us and told us to check out the classified section of the newspaper. He said that he would return the next day to check on us. The next day when Jimmy got off work he came over to check on us again. This time he went straight to the refrigerator. He said, "No food." He asked if Ms Conti had been home. While our words said yes our expressions said otherwise. Jimmy told me that he talked to Daddy and Daddy instructed him to bring me home if our situation hadn't changed. We begged Jimmy to tell Daddy that we were okay but he insisted that I pack my bags. Alease said, "if you are going home, I am going with you. We packed our bags and Jimmy took us back home to Virginia.

I joined my mother working down in the country, leaving Front Royal at four in the morning. I reported to the Staffing Agency for my daily assignment at six-thirty in the morning. After several weeks, I began getting my assignments the day before, therefore I could get started earlier and get off earlier. Sometimes, my employer would pick me up at the Drug Fair parking lot in Falls Church, Virginia. Other times I would take the bus to my place of work or Momma's driver would drop me off at my place of work prior to arriving at the Drug Fair in Falls Church. It all depended on where in the northern Virginia area I was assigned to work. This was all new to me. I had never rode public transportation but I did not have any problems finding my way around.

On my very first assignment to clean a house, I took the bus. When I arrived at my place of work and rang the doorbell, one of the boys came to the door. I said, "Good morning, I'm the maid." He began yelling for his mother as if something was wrong. Soon the whole family was at the door starring at me. The lady of the house, without even saying good morning, asked, "How old are you?" I said, "I am eighteen, ma'am." She said, "I apologize for having you stand outside the door, please come in." She said, "You look twelve." I assured her that I was eighteen and that I had been sent by the Staffing Agency to clean her house. She introduced herself and then introduced me to the family, her husband and two sons twelve and fifteen. Her twelve-year-old son followed me around all day helping me dust, getting the vacuum cleaner out and returning it to the closet and getting the cleaning supplies out for me. Every time I turned around he was under foot trying to help. I never had such attention when trying to do a job.

Momma said that you couldn't let the white folks know all of our cleaning secrets. Momma taught me to use (Pledge) furniture polish in the bathroom and in the kitchen to make the washbasin, tub and appliances shine after they were thoroughly cleaned. I had to use the same tricks on my employer's son that I used on my little brother to get rid of him while I put the finishing touches on my cleaning. I told him that I heard his mother calling him. I also told him that I had to shut the door to the bathroom because I needed some privacy. He sat outside the bathroom door and waited patiently for me to open the door.

At lunchtime, the lady of the house made lunch and I sat with the family and had my lunch too. When I finished cleaning the house, the lady told me that her regular lady took two days to do what I did in a single day. She said that she had not seen her twelve-year-old son take such an interest in cleaning the house. She gave me an extra two dollars in addition to my normal pay of twelve dollars, I earned more money that day than Momma. I was also hired to come back every week on Wednesday.

When I told Momma that I had fourteen dollars because the lady gave me two extra dollars because her regular lady took two days to do what I did in one, Momma and the older ladies in the car pool schooled me on working too fast. Ms. Hazel injected her words of wisdom, "If the house has more than three bedrooms and two baths and you change the beds, it's a good days work. You should make sure that you can't complete the work in eight hours and you should get extra for working beyond the eight hours." Another one of the ladies chimed in, "For God's sake, never tell your employer that you do windows." She reiterated, "You don't do windows." Now, you repeat after me, "I don't do windows. The men get five dollars an hour for doing windows." I repeated, "I don't do windows. The men get five dollars an hour for doing windows." They all laughed.

The best jobs were the ones where the lady of the house wasn't home and I finished early. I couldn't get accustomed to working slow. I wasn't interested in the stories and I didn't work with the TV on. I liked leaving early and riding the bus to learn my way around or going shopping.

One of my jobs was in Fairfax, Virginia. Fairfax was situated on our route about ten miles before we got to Falls Church. The driver dropped me off in Fairfax on his way to Falls Church and picked me up on his way back as they were heading home. I walked to and from the main drag to my place of employment. This lady had a big house. Because I got there early and left late, she always paid extra. I liked working at the big houses because I had to organize, work fast and I made extra money. This lady worked outside the home and I liked having the house all to myself. She gave me her clothes that she could no longer wear or no longer wanted. She had good taste in clothes and most of the clothes fit perfectly. Momma would say, "If someone wants to give you something, take it even if you have to throw it away as soon as you get out of their sight. Just take it! Someday they may give you something good." We called the bags of stuff, "goodie bags." Goodie bags were often a topic of discussion, exchange and bartering on the way home in the evenings.

One day as I stood along the roadside waiting for my ride, this guy drove past driving a maroon Pontiac. He circled around, drove back to where I was standing, parked his car, walked over to me and introduced himself. He said, "Hello, my name is George Gibson, do you need a ride?" I said, "No my ride will be along shortly." He asked, "Are you married?" I giggled and said, "No." Finally, my ride pulled up to the curb. George asked, "What's your name?" As I was walking away, I said, "Betty Kilby." As we pulled off, Mr. George Gibson pulled off behind us. All the ladies in the car were interested in who was this tall, handsome young man. They kept looking back to see when he turned around to go back towards Falls Church. As we neared Front Royal, the excitement turned to anxiety because I knew that I would be in trouble. Momma was very quiet and I could see the dissatisfaction look on her face. Even though I was eighteen, I was treated like I was thirteen. The fiasco in D.C. didn't help much in proving that I was capable of making my own decisions.

As we pulled into the Tastee Freeze parking lot, Daddy was there to pick us up and George pulled into the parking lot too. I got out of the car and walked over to George's car. I asked, "What the hell you think you are doing?" He said, "You left so fast that I didn't get your phone number or any contact information." I grabbed my head in distress and asked George to wait minute. I walked back over to my father and asked if I could ride to Happy Creek to the house with George. By this time Momma had given Daddy the scoop on how George followed us home. Daddy wouldn't let me ride to the house with George, however he did say that George could follow us to home and we could visit at the house. I walked back over to George's car and said, "Well, you followed me this far, come on and follow me home." He said, "Why don't you ride with me?" I said, "It don't work that way today, you are a stranger." I went over to Daddy's car, got in and we drove off. Sure enough, George followed us to Happy Creek. We sat outside in the yard and talked until dinner was ready. Patty came outside and said, "Momma wants to know if the young man is going home or is he staying for dinner?" I asked what were we having. The very first thing she said was cabbage and I frowned. I could imagine the house stinking from the cabbage. George said, "Would you like to go out to eat?" I chuckled to myself because Front Royal was not D.C. Then I replied, "You are still a stranger." He asked, "Can I stay for dinner, I like cabbage." I told Pat to tell Momma that George was staying for dinner.

During dinner, Momma and Daddy played the fifty million questions game. Where do you live? Who are your parents? Where do they go to church? Where do they work? Where do you work? He was much older than the boys who had visited me at the house in the past. He answered their questions without hesitation. He was not intimidated. He was quite impressive, however Momma and Daddy were cautious because no one in their circle of friends or acquaintances knew anything about this George Gibson.

It was my turn to do the dishes and I knew the drill. George helped me to do the dishes. We retired to the living room. I explained that my parents were strict and old fashioned and that they still dictated my life. I told him about my brother bringing me home from D.C. I explained that to go out in the car with him would still require my Daddy's approval and would probably require that my sister come along too. He asked if I was telling the truth about being eighteen. I showed him my driver's license to prove that I was eighteen. He wanted to come back the next day, but I declined. I needed some time to figure out the house rules since I had graduated from high school.

That Saturday, I asked Daddy about going out to the movies with George the following Saturday evening. He agreed but I had to take my fifteen-year-old sister, Patty with us. Patty had learned to play the game quite well. She refused to go unless we took her friend Mary Cecil with us. I was so angry at the idea of being eighteen, having so little freedom and no hope for changes in the future. I hated the idea that the boys didn't have to go through all this crap. I accepted Daddy's and Patty's terms because at this point in my life it was their way or no way.

Daddy extended my curfew to midnight after I graduated; however guests visiting me at the house had to leave by eleven in the evening. If my guest didn't leave by eleven, I would hear the clock alarm go off. Next Daddy would come through the living room and walk slowly up the steps with his bare feet clearing his throat and mumbling as he took the sixteen steps leading upstairs to the bathroom. He put his work pants on over his pajamas. If my guest was still there when he came down the steps from the bathroom, he would ask, "Betty, is that young man planning to spend the night?" I would answer, "No sir, Daddy, he is leaving now." I tried very hard not to make Daddy get up, but some time, I would forget or just let the devil get into me.

I met George in the Drug Fair parking lot after I got off work that Monday. I could not wait to get off work to make my way back to the parking lot to meet my new friend. I knew it would not look good for me to be sitting in his car when Momma got to Drug Fair so we went in and sat in a booth in the restaurant section of Drug Fair. Every time I sat down in a restaurant, I thought about the time we were refused service at Belle Boyd in Front Royal. Every time I got around George, I was so excited that I had a hard time eating. If we were going to sit in the restaurant, I had to order something so I ordered ice cream. It was one of my favorite foods and there were so many flavors.

I saw George everyday after I got off work. Sometimes he would pick me up from work, other times we would meet somewhere other than the Falls Church Drug Fair. If he picked me up at work, he dropped me off at the bus stop. I would walk over to the Drug Fair because I knew that I was not allowed to be in the car with him alone. Sometimes I would pretend to work on Mondays and spend the day with him. George worked Tuesday through Saturday and was off on Mondays. He would take me over into D.C. to have lunch at a restaurant where we could sit down since I had such a fascination with sit-down restaurants. He took me to the zoo for the first time. We went to the museums. We even went to the beach one Monday. He gave my life meaning. He made me smile and feel special. I enjoyed the freedom of meeting George in Falls Church. I felt like a woman and not a child.

George's family was not church people, however George went to church with our family. Most of the time he drove us to church, my little brother and my little sister would ride with us. Sometimes he would jokingly tease me; by saying, "I'm coming up to do the family thing."

One time Daddy let me go to a dance with George after I negotiated, begged, fought and got my butt whipped for sassing. When I asked to go to the dance with George, Daddy suggested that I meet George at the dance while he took me to the dance and waited for me outside like he did when I was in high school. I told Daddy if that was the way it had to be I wouldn't go at all. Then I blew up, lost control. I said, "I'm sick and tired of being treated like a child. I might as well be dead. You destroyed my life because old man Dick Finks took your land." Before I could get another word out, I saw the veins in his forehead protruding, his tongue was rolled where you could see the blue veins, his eyes were blazing and his belt was in his hand. He yelled, "Sassing, I'll teach you to sass, for as long as you live in my house you will live by my rules." I had welts all over my legs and I was too stubborn to cry and that made my beating much worse. Life was closing in on me. My physical wounds healed from the beating. I was able to conceal the welts left by the belt from George. Daddy ended-up letting me ride to the dance with George. George got me home just as the alarm went off signaling the stroke of midnight. George poked fun at me by calling me Cinderella. I thought to myself, all Cinderella had to do was work. I had to take a beating.

George was growing impatient and began pressuring me for sex. His birthday was August twenty-first. I promised to take off and spend the day with him on his birthday. We went to his brother's house. We had the house all to ourselves. I cooked lunch for him and we made love for the first time that day. I was feeling quite confident and I let him drop me off in the Falls Church Drug Fair parking lot. I didn't realize it but he put a hickey on my neck. As soon as I walked into Drug Fair, Ms. Hazel Washington said, "I know what you been doing today." I said, "What?" She said, "You have a hickey on you neck and that can mean only one thing, you been screwing around." I thought, "How could a man who proclaimed to love me do such a thing? How could I conceal this from Momma, Daddy and the commuters riding in the car?" I was panicking! Ms. Hazel had a goodie bag with an outfit that the woman she worked for had given her for her daughter. She said, "Let's go in the bathroom and see if it will fit and cover up that hickey." It fit and it covered up the hickey. She told me to keep the outfit. I walked out of Drug Fair and walked over to George. He was bragging to his friend about busting my cherry. I walked over and slapped him as hard as I could. I heard him calling me as I walked away but I didn't turn around. I went straight to the car and got in.

It was all I could do to maintain my composure on the journey home. I closed my eyes and pretended to sleep. My mind kept remembering the day that I was raped by the three white boys. They wanted to violate a Nigger and George wanted a notch in his belt. I knew that sex without marriage was a sin. I kept thinking why me Lord? What have I done to deserve such punishment? I knew that I had sinned and this was my punishment.

Ms. Hazel knew that Momma would figure out that I wasn't wearing that same yellow dress that I had on that morning. On the way home Ms. Hazel told the other riders that she didn't believe me when I told her that I could wear a children-size fourteen dress and that she had bet the dress and lost the dress to me. I didn't open my eyes or say a word.

George kept calling me on the phone and trying to talk to me at the Drug Fair but I refused to see or talk to him. I pretended that nothing had happened between us, it was the only way that I could survive.

George showed up at my house one day when I didn't go to work and I was home alone. I opened the inside door but not the screen door. He said that I looked at him as though I looked straight through him. He begged for forgiveness. He told me that he loved me. He said that it was a man-thing to brag about their love affairs. I had no words for him because he no longer existed in my mind. He called me "a cold-hearted bitch with my religion up my ass because I didn't have the capacity to forgive."

On the third Sunday in September, I was ready to go to Flint Hill to church with the family. Jimmy pulled into the yard. He was going to Millwood church for their homecoming. He was dating one of my girlfriends, Pearline Washington, and he wanted me to go to church with him. Daddy let me go. Pearline and I were walking down the country road in front of the church when this car drove past. I took notice of the driver of the car and he looked good to me. The guys in the car must have noticed us, too. They made a u-turn in the road and came back to us and stopped. Pearline introduced me to Andrew Fisher. We took to each other right away. Andrew parked in the church parking lot and walked up to where we were standing at the back entrance to the church. I wanted to go into the church and have lunch but Andrew wanted me to stay outside and talk to him. I asked Andrew if he could afford to buy me a soda and a country ham sandwich, he answered, "Yes." Then I asked Andrew if he was going to have lunch with me. He said, "I think I can handle that." Jimmy came over to get Pearline to have lunch with him inside the church. Andrew bought the sodas and sandwiches and we sat in his car and had lunch. Andrew wanted to just sit and talk because he was tired. He was out until four in the morning partying. His mother made him get up early to drive her to church.

I was wearing a winter white mohair coat with a gold velvet collar. The mohair from my coat shed onto Andrew's dark suit. We spent the day talking. We shared stories about being different. Andrew was adopted and had more white features than colored.

I told the story of our attempt to be served lunch at the Belle Boyd restaurant and Andrew told his story about being served at the lunch counter at the Trailway Bus Station. He said, after he had sat at the counter and dined sufficiently, he ordered a sandwich and drink for his mother "to go." The waiter brought his "to-go" box and the check. Before he could pay the check, his mother came up to him and the waiter heard Andrew call this colored woman Momma. The waiter realized that he had served this colored boy at the counter. He got so excited that he chased them out of the restaurant without charging them for the meals. We laughed at how funny it was that white people could get so excited about serving this little colored boy and the very act that brought him into existence looking as white as any white person was so much more intimate than being served at the lunch counter.

I talked about how I imagined old man Dick Finks taking my grandma Kilby in the kitchen. We came up with the idea and coined the phrase "kitchen baby." I reached in my purse and pulled out my ballpoint pen. I explained that the pen was my magic wand. I gently tapped Andrew on the head three times and said, "I dub you and all the babies born of colored mothers conceived by the white master during and after slavery special babies and these babies shall be called kitchen babies. They shall be blessed because their mothers suffered. You are special! Andrew reached over, smiled, pinched my cheek and said, "You are a nut."

The day went by in flash and Jimmy was ready to go home because he had to drive back to D.C. that night. Andrew was leaving for college the following Monday morning. I gave him my address and phone number. We promised each other that we would write each other that night. I held out my finger and we did the pinky swear. I wrote Andrew that night thanking him for lunch and a wonderful day. Sure enough, I got a letter on Wednesday postmarked on Monday from Petersburg, Virginia. Andrew wrote in his letter to me that he decided not to get his suit cleaned because every time he looked at the mohair on his suit, he thought about me.

We wrote to each other at least twice a week. I was happy again. I liked having a friend.

I had not given George a second thought until I missed my period. The virus that caused me to throw-up in the mornings didn't go away. I wrote to my new friend Andrew and I told him about George and having missed my period. I told him that I would understand if he didn't want to write to me any more. He wrote back to me saying, "My love is not like a water faucet whereby I can cut it off at will, I think I love you." He suggested that I go to the doctor and verify the pregnancy. I was afraid that my parents might find out so I didn't go to the doctor. I prayed that I wasn't pregnant.

Andrew was coming home for Thanksgiving and I was excited about seeing him again. My child was three months in the making and I had already fallen in love with my baby. Barbara Jackson and I had talked about getting married and having children. We even had names for our children. My little girl was going to be named Bettina. That was my Spanish name. My little boy was going to be named Tony. I never thought about the possibility of having a child out of wedlock. I hadn't gained much weight, but my eighteen-inch waistline was gone. I still hadn't told my parents or been to see the doctor. Andrew called me as soon as he arrived in Middleburg, Virginia. I told him I was home sick. Thirty-eight minutes later he showed up at my door. When I looked at the clock, I asked, "What did you do? Fly up here?" He kissed me and I melted like butter on a hot stove. He rubbed my stomach and I thanked God for putting this kind and gentle man in my life.

Andrew joined us for Thanksgiving dinner and he invited me to the movies on Friday night. Andrew already knew that Patty and Mary Cecil would be joining us at the movie. Andrew's twenty-first birthday was that Saturday and he was going to New York on the train with his parents or at least that's what he told me. His parents hosted a surprise birthday party for him. Since his mother didn't know about me, I wasn't invited to his birthday party. Andrew told me about the party the next day. He apologized for my not being invited. He said, "I am kind of glad that you weren't invited. My mother and Joe invited every girl that I ever dated and they all thought the invitation meant something. I spent most of the time thinking about you and trying to avoid my former girlfriends. If you had been there you probably would be mad at me too." I hugged him without saying a word thinking that if I was a good and unselfish woman I would send him away because I was a disgrace to my family and I would bring shame upon him too.

Andrew visited with me before he returned to school. He made me promise to tell my parents about the baby and to go to the doctor. I hated for the holidays to end.

I found a doctor in Falls Church and he verified that I was pregnant. He prescribed prenatal vitamins but I was afraid to buy them out of fear that my parents might see them and find out about the pregnancy. I was healthy. I ate plenty of vegetables and I really didn't understand the need for vitamins. I did not make any appointments for follow-up visits. I told the nurse that I would make an appointment with my regular doctor.

I got an assignment to take care of the Perkins's baby for a week while the Perkins went out of town. I told my sister Pat that I was pregnant. I wrote a letter to my parents that simply said, "I am pregnant, I'm sorry." I asked Pat to give the note to Mom and Dad after I left for the Perkins's assignment. I thought this would allow time for them to get use to the idea that I was pregnant and cool off while I was gone. Since Momma didn't work on Saturdays, I planned my return on Saturday. That way, I wouldn't have to go through this dreaded ordeal but once. I dreaded going home that Saturday. I felt so alone, helpless and dirty. They picked me up that Saturday at the Tastee Freeze. Ms. Hazel rode to Happy Creek with us. The minute we drove off after Ms. Hazel got out of the car, Momma asked, "Are you pregnant?" I said, "Yes." Momma asked, "Who is the father?" Immediately I had visions of Daddy with the shotgun forcing me to marry George. I responded with the worst possible answer, "I don't know." Momma called me a whore and all the names appropriate for someone who had brought such disgrace upon the family and the Kilby name. I responded by saying, "I know, I understand how you feel." Being called a whore was better than being forced to marry a man who used me like the white boys who raped me. Momma suggested that I be sent to Aunt Polly's and that I would give my baby up for adoption. I really made a bad situation worse because I exploded and blamed them for turning me into this monster. I told them that I would die before I gave away my baby. We fought all the time. Daddy couldn't whip me because he was afraid that he might hurt the baby. I would rather have been beaten than watch the disappointment on Daddy's face or hear the disappointment and harshness of Momma's tone.

During the Christmas holiday Andrew took me home to meet his family. By this time Andrew's mother knew that I was pregnant. Andrew wanted me to say that the baby that I was carrying was his baby but I wouldn't let him.

As soon as Andrew's mother was alone with me she asked, "Is that Andrew's baby? If it is his baby, I want to take care of it." I answered, "No it's not Andrew's baby. We have not been together that way. I met Andrew before I realized that I was pregnant." She asked, "What about the baby's father?" I said, "He doesn't know and if I have my way about it he will never know." She asked, "Why?" I reflected on the memory of him bragging on how he busted my cherry and him trying to apologize. I was off in a daze when I heard Mrs. Fisher asking, "Is there a good reason for not telling the father?" As I regained my composure, I said, "He was a mistake, end of the subject." She said, "My son has feelings for you, what are your plans?" I said, "I have no idea. I'll work it out."

Even though I was four months pregnant, I still wasn't showing. For the first time, I was allowed to go to the movies without having to take my little sister. I still had to be home before midnight and my company had to leave by eleven at night.

The Christmas holidays were over and my only friend went back to school. As I grew bigger and bigger, people began to talk. Momma and Daddy discouraged me from going to church or out in public. I cried as they drove off to church leaving me home in disgrace. I didn't know how much longer I would be allowed to live at home. I worked as much as I could and saved as much money as I could. I tried to conceal my love for my baby because it only angered Mom and Dad and they believed that I got pregnant out of spite.

One day while I was home alone sick as usual, George showed up. He was as non-existent to me as he was the last time he showed up at the door. He made it just about as far as he did the last time, to the screen door. He looked at me and said jokingly, "Are you pregnant or are you just fat?" I responded with, "None of your business." He said, "It's my business if that's my baby you are carrying." I said, "It's not your baby" and shut the door. He yelled, "Bitch" and he walked away. I sat on the steps leading upstairs for hours trying to understand my coldness. What turned me into this cruel, evil witch who could not forgive George. I had heard my brothers talking in the same manner about girls that they had been with for sex and for love. Was I truly crazy? Was I possessed by the Devil? Did I bring all this misery upon myself? Was I being punished for always reminding Daddy about losing his land to old man Dick Finks? I knew that the reminder would hurt him deeply. I was evil and stupid. Stupid! Stupid! Stupid! God have mercy on my wicked soul.

One night Momma, Daddy and I were having that same argument about sending me to Aunt Polly's and giving my baby up for adoption. The telephone rang and Patty answered the phone. It was Andrew. Patty told Andrew that Momma and Daddy were going to send me to Aunt Polly's and they were going to make me give my baby up for adoption. By the time I answered the phone I could barely talk from crying. Andrew said, "Don't try to talk. Just listen. My Easter break is three weeks away. I am coming home for Easter and we are going to get married. You don't have to do anything with me; you don't even have to stay married to me if you don't want to stay married. We are going to give that baby a name. You can live with my parents until we decide what we are going to do. All I want to hear right now is yes. Do you think you can just say yes?" I said, "Yes." He said, "Now say yes I will marry you." I said, "Yes, I will marry you." He asked, "Are you alright now?" I asked, "Are you sure you want to do this?" He said, "I am not going to stand by and let the love of my life slip away from me. I love you and I want to be with you forever." We said our good-byes and I hung up the phone.

I didn't want to spoil the moment so I went straight to bed. Andrew had rode in on the white horse and saved my baby and me. The next morning I announced that I was getting married on March 29, 1964. I knew the rules and I accepted my shame. I contracted with Ms. Pearl Jordan to make my wedding dress, a light blue maternity dress. I asked Aunt Nellie Alsberry to make my wedding cake. Andrew's mother made all of the other arrangements. Andrew had asked that we have a small ceremony with a few friends for the benefit of his mother since he was an only child and his mother wanted to do something.

A couple of days later, I received a beautiful letter from Andrew putting his proposal in writing. The letter started with, "love is magic pure and sweet, for it alone makes life complete, given freely never bought; the gift mankind had always sought." This man had to be sent to me from God.

Andrew came to see me as soon as he got home from school. He was taking Barbering Education in school. He told his classmates that he was getting married and he needed money for the rings. He must have cut every man's hair at Virginia State College because in those three weeks he earned enough money to buy the wedding ring set. I was not expecting a ring. I had to go out and buy a wedding band. When we went to get the marriage license, Daddy went with us. Daddy was so anxious to get me married; he paid for the license. They probably thought Andrew was the father of my baby because I stuck with the I don't know who the father is, I never told them any different. Only my baby brother Gene, Momma, Daddy and one of the children from my Sunday School class attended the wedding.

Andrew went back to school the day after we got married. I stayed with his parents as planned. I started going to the clinic for prenatal care. At this stage in my pregnancy, I had not had any prenatal care. Andrew came home from school in anticipation of Bettina's or Tony's arrival. I went into labor on Saturday afternoon. Bettina Sylvia Fisher was born on Sunday afternoon, May 17, 1964. On her birth certificate we put Andrew T. Fisher as father. Andrew vowed to care for her and love her for as long as she lived. She was beautiful and I vowed to love her for as long as I lived because she saved my life. Andrew was the sweetest, kindest, most gentle man that I have ever known. He saved my life and the life of my child. I vowed to love him forever. Andrew went back to school that following Monday morning.

Eleven months later, April 29, 1965 we had another baby girl, Renée Andrea Fisher. Andrew did not see his second baby for six weeks. Andrew graduated from college in 1968 and went into the Army as a Commissioned Officer. He was truly an Officer and a gentleman. We moved to Ft. Bragg, North Carolina, and lived in military housing. We had the most wonderful six months of our lives. We were so poor I washed clothes by hand. At the end of the month we were trading food with friends and neighbors to make a complete meal. We were rich with love and happiness. I followed Andrew around like a piece of gum stuck to his shoe. We walked in the rain and didn't mind getting wet. We were so close that when I got pregnant again with baby number three, Andrew had all the morning sickness, tardiness and weight gain.

We thought the good times would last forever but they didn't. Andrew got orders for Vietnam. He got a thirty-day leave that started the first week of December and ended the first week of January. He was scheduled to go to jungle training in Panama for two weeks prior to going to Vietnam. I didn't want him to go because he was a "sole surviving son." Andrew's father had made the military his career and had instilled a strong sense of duty into Andrew.

After being out on our own, I didn't want to go back to live with either his parents or my parents. My parents agreed to let us park a trailer on the property next door to the main house. The Army taught Andrew to establish good credit by buying small items on credit and paying off the loan on payday. Luckily, Andrew had good credit. We bought a trailer. The salesman knocked a $1,000 off the price of the trailer because Andrew was in the military, then he said, "If you buy this trailer today, I will throw in the clothes dryer." I asked, "Does that mean that a washer will come with this trailer? A dryer is no good without a washer." He seemed surprised that there was not a washer in the trailer. He thought for a minute and said, "You make a good point. Oh, what the heck, this boy is going off to defend his country, I'll throw in the washer too." I said, "What about these steps, do they come with the trailer." He said, "The steps are twenty-eight dollars a set. Let me add twenty-eight dollars to the contract and I will give you two sets of steps for the price of one. One set for the back and one for the front." We agreed. During the thirty days of leave, Andrew got the trailer set-up with water, sewer and electricity. Andrew's parents were angry because we didn't come back to live with them so they did not help. They even took us off their Christmas gift list.

On Christmas Eve, we went to this hardware store to buy some plumbing supplies. I spotted this small Christmas tree; I asked what are you going to do with that tree? The store attendant looked at me pregnant and the pretty little girls standing beside me and he said surprisingly, "You don't have a tree yet." I said, "No, my husband got orders to go to Vietnam and the money is funny." He gave us the tree with decorations and all. He took the tree to the car for us and said, "Merry Christmas." We had won a couple of stuffed toys at the carnival when we were at Ft. Bragg that I had put away. We put them under the tree for the girls.

My brother Bubble was working for Giant Food and he gave us a toaster for Christmas. We took the toaster back to Giant's and used the credit to buy food. We had a wonderful Christmas; my family was generous with their Christmas giving. We had Christmas dinner with my family. Naturally, we took leftovers home.

In early January, Andrew left for jungle training. For the first time in my life, I was on my own with the awesome responsibility of house, bills and children. Andrew always managed the checkbook. In anticipation of the check, he listed the check in the check register. When the check came, I added the check to the register and wrote the bills. I was still showing a balance when I got a call from the bank informing me that I was overdrawn. I panicked. I carried my checkbook to the bank and they helped me to find the error. I could not catch up on the bills until the following month. The overdrawn check was written to Warren Paint and Supply and they agreed to forgo a payment that month because they had a good relationship with my

Daddy. I had to be very careful with the spending until the next month. I carefully evaluated the inventory of food to make sure that my kids wouldn't go hungry. It was tough but we made it through the month.

Andrew was able to come home for a couple of days after he finished his jungle training. He had the most beautiful tan and no tan lines anywhere on his body. I raided Momma and Daddy's cupboards to make sure that Andrew had a feast before going off to Vietnam. I took some cream from one of the milk cans. I knew that taking the cream off the milk would lower the value of the milk but Daddy agreed that it was a good cause. I shook the cream in a half-gallon jar until it turned to butter. I used the butter and buttermilk to make Andrew's favorite pound cake flavored with lemon and almond extract.

When Andrew got ready to leave for Vietnam, I told him that he would not be in Vietnam for his full term. I said, "When this baby gets ready to come into this world, you will have the labor pains and the Army will have to ship you home." He left for Vietnam January 23, 1969.

When we were stationed in Ft. Bragg, the more senior military wives schooled me on what to expect when Andrew went to Vietnam. They described what the vehicle would look like, how the telegram would read if Andrew got wounded. Bettina, Renée and I went over to Aunt Alice's that day. Bettina had a loose tooth and Aunt Alice pulled the tooth because I was scared to pull the tooth. It was exciting because it was Bettina's first tooth. Momma called me at Aunt Alice's and asked me to come home. It was February 28, 1969. When I approached the driveway and saw that black sedan, I knew that Andrew had been hit. I knew the telegram would say that he had been seriously wounded. I got myself and the girls out of the car. Before the officer finish reading the telegram, my legs buckled under me and they went limp like they did so often when I wanted to die.

I woke-up in the emergency room of Warren Memorial Hospital. I couldn't die I had responsibilities, children who needed me and loved me. I did not have enough happiness and goodness in my life to lose my soul mate now. God's promise that for every bad day we would have equal amount of good days had not fully materialized, I had more good days coming to me. I pulled myself together to be strong for my children and Andrew. I had to be there for Andrew like he was there for me when I got pregnant with Bettina.

Three days passed and I had not heard anything from anyone. I went to the mailbox and there was no letter. I drove to the Post Office and asked the clerk to check to see if there was any mail for me. There was nothing. I couldn't be strong any longer. I sat in the car and cried, the small hands from the back of the car touched me on the back and so gently said, "It will be alright Mommy." Aunt Liz, Uncle Bob's wife came over to the car and she prayed for Andrew and our family. She said everything would be alright. She asked, "Are you going to be okay, you have those pretty little girls with you." I said, "I will be okay, I don't know what I would do without my little angels."

I remembered the Red Cross and stopped by the Red Cross office. Later that evening the Red Cross called me at my Mother's because we could not afford a phone. They described his wounds, told me that he was resting comfortably and that I should get a letter within a couple of days. I got a letter a few days later that was not in Andrew's handwriting.

Andrew arrived at Walter Reed on March 23, 1969. My doctor told me not to drive to Washington, D.C. because I could go into labor anytime. The baby was due April 29. I called around for two hours to find someone to drive me to D.C. When I ran out of people to call, I said a prayer, got in the car and drove to D.C. When I got to Walter Reed, I couldn't find a parking space. I got frustrated, the more frustrated I became the more the baby pushed up against my rib cage. At last, I found a parking space. We located Andrew's room, the children weren't permitted in the hospital room, but Bettina and Renée were such good children the nurses let them stay. The first thing Andrew said was, "You were right, you said I would be back in time for the baby." I said, "This is not what I had in mind, but I'll keep you." He was in good spirits but he had lost so much weight. He said he had enough blood transfusions to replenish his whole blood supply. His left leg was broken. He had a gash in his back about six inches long and it had a tube draining out the fluids from the wound in his back. He had stitches from his navel to the bottom of his stomach. There was a big gash in his left arm. Some of the nurses said, "Don't look at the wounds because it would mark the baby," but the doctor showed it to me anyway to help me to understand. The wound on his arm looked like a cheese pizza.

Andrew was concerned because I drove to D.C. contrary to the doctor's orders. I told Andrew that God was with me. Andrew's parents took Bettina and Renée until Erika was born. I stayed with my brother Jimmy, his wife and their two-month-old daughter. I rode the city bus to the hospital. My brother Bubble would pick me up from Walter Reed; take me to dinner and back to Jimmy's at ten o'clock at night.

Erika was born at Walter Reed on April 25, 1969. My water broke while I was waiting in the pharmacy to get a prescription filled. I left a trail of water from the pharmacy to the delivery room on the third floor. By the time I got to the delivery room and to the bed my stomach was vibrating. In less than an hour, Erika entered this world. Andrew couldn't come up to be with me and I didn't see him for two days. We were so close, yet so far apart. My sister Pat was attending Howard University. She was right down the street. Both Jimmy and Bubble were at work. Things were happening so fast, I didn't have time to call them and I went to sleep right after the delivery. I woke up in the middle of the night, alone and lonely.

The doctors grafted tissue to the injury on Andrew's arm with the intent of grafting nerves to that part of his body. They cut a flap from his side and attached it to his arm. For six weeks he had a body cast on his entire chest area with his arm attached to his side in order for tissue to grow on his arm. He slept on a frame bed so that he could be rotated daily. He was so miserable in that condition that when the body cast was removed, he said it was not worth it to have more surgeries that may or may not restore total use to his hand. When he went in for the surgery to detach the flap from his side and arm, they took skin from his leg to put on the arm. He didn't realize that the nerves for his arm would be taken from other parts of his body.

At this point he had lost interest in teaching Barbering Education or opening a chain of Barber Shops. Even if the nerve damage in his hand could be restored he had one leg shorter than the other that would make it hard for him to stand for long periods of time. Barbers must be able to stand for long periods of time.

After six months in the hospital, Andrew got a pass to go home for a week. On the way to pick him up from the hospital, the car broke down. Knocking, sputtering and backfiring, I was able to drive to a gas station. The station attendant told me that the car needed some work. I called Andrew at the hospital and told him about the car breaking down. He told me to leave the car and get a rent a car. The gas station attendant let me use the phone. I went down the list in the yellow pages. The rental car companies turned me down one by one because I wasn't twenty-five years old. When I got to the last rental car company I began to tell my story. "Please listen to me before you turn me down because I am not twenty-five years old. My husband was wounded in Vietnam; he has been in the hospital six months. Today will be the first time he will be able to come home for a visit with his three little girls and me. My car broke down on the way to the hospital. Please help me! You are the last company on this list. If you don't rent me a car my husband won't be able to come home. The credit card is in his name, he is twenty-five years old. Please help me." The man replied, "My son is in Vietnam now. Where are you?" I gave him the address. He said, "I will be right up to pick you up." He came to pick me up in a car that looked like my car. When I got in the car I said, "There are only minor differences between this car and my car." He asked, "What year is your vehicle?" I said, "1968." He said, "Your car should still be under warranty." When we got back to his office, he called one of his friends at the Chevrolet dealership and talked to him about my situation. As it turned out my car could be repaired under warranty. He made arrangements for the dealership to pick-up my car. I called the gas station and informed the attendant that the car dealership would pick-up my car and repair under warranty. The mechanic charged me fifty dollars because he said they had already started the repairs. I was so grateful that God had put that wonderful man from the car rental agency in my life, I paid the fifty bucks and vowed that I would not be taken advantage of in such a manner again. One of my Dad's philosophies was, "You live to learn and die to forget it all."

I finally made it to the hospital in the rental car, picked Andrew up and we went home. My brother Gene was on hand to help me get Andrew in the house. The wound in his back was still open and susceptible to infection. I had to irrigate the wound everyday to fight off infection. That was one of the conditions of the release. I was very careful not to let the wound get infected. It was easier caring for Andrew at home rather than making the seventy-five-mile journey everyday to Walter Reed Hospital with three little children who weren't suppose to be in the hospital room.

During the next round of emergencies, I was called to come back to the hospital because Andrew's fever was so high that he may not make it through the night. I made the long commute, trying to provide babysitters for three children, fighting with the nurses to keep my children with me while I sat and held my husband's hand and prayed that God would not send the death angel to take him from me. In the midst of all this, I got pregnant again. My only comeback was, not knowing whether he would live threw another day, and he got whatever he wanted, whenever and however. Besides Andrew told me not to worry, he said, "My sperm is so weak from the surgeries and x-rays, there was no way I could get you pregnant." I believed him. Wrong!

When he wanted to get away from all the pain and agony, I drove the car right up to the emergency room door, loaded him in the car and drove right pass the guard with Andrew still in his pajamas. We drove all over D.C. and visited our D.C. relatives. Sometimes they were home and sometimes we just used their home as a resting place. Andrew was so proud of the fact that he survived Vietnam, came back and conceived his son after having three girls.

Andrew Tony Fisher was born on July 13, 1970. It was our first baby that Andrew was there at the hospital, waiting outside the delivery room for the arrival of his first son. The nurse brought this little blond hair white baby over and handed him to me. I said, "You have given me the wrong baby, there must be some mistake." She looked at Andrew and she looked at me and said, "Mrs. Fisher this is the only baby in the delivery room." Andrew took the baby from the nurse and brought him over to the bed. He said, "You don't know what genes are lurking in the background of a "kitchen baby." We both laughed and counted all the fingers and toes.

Our family was like a rose garden, beautiful and colorful. Bettina and Erika were beautiful children a shade browner than me with beautiful long dark brown hair. I parted the hair down the middle with a ponytail on each side. Renée and Tony had more white features and were fair complexion like their father. Renée's hair was auburn and was styled like her sisters with two ponytails. Tony's blond hair was styled like John Kennedy Jr. Some people would stare at us. Some people would assume that I was babysitting the children and said things like, "How long have you been taking care of the children?" Some people would ask, "Are all these children related?" We had a lot of fun saying, "These children are all descendants of "kitchen babies." We waited for these people to say, "What are kitchen babies?" I said. "They are babies born to colored mothers conceived by the white master to slaves and former slaves, colored women conceiving children along with their kitchen responsibilities." Some of the people commented, but most people took off as if they were sorry for their curiosity. Andrew got embarrassed.

Andrew was declared one-hundred-percent disabled by the Army and he was medically discharged. I declared that I would encourage, support and nurse him back to a full and productive life but I would never be totally dependent upon him or anyone else ever again. Had he died from his wounds, I would have been pitiful with no job-skills to support my children and no life-skills to survive the people who prey on the ignorant and misinformed.

Chapter 5 _____

Harsh Realities

The interview was like a roller coaster ride at Six Flags.
I was at an all time high when I thought I was doing good until
the consultant told me that there was no doubt that I could and would
do a good job but the roller coaster made a sudden drop when
the consultant said that his direction was to go out and
find someone who had already developed
the best practices. I wondered why I was there.

Andrew recovered from his wounds and went back to school at the local college, Lord Fairfax Community College. June 1972, he graduated Magna Cum Laude with an Associates Degree in Merchandise Management. He got a job as a Manager Trainee at W.T. Grants. Bettina and Renée were in elementary school.

It was time for me to get my life together. Andrew didn't want me to go to work, but I was determined to stand on my own two feet. He wanted that same little girl that he left behind when he went to Vietnam. She was gone; she grew up. I longed for that kind and gentle young man that I married but the war had hardened and matured him too. He had nightmares and he became withdrawn. Our fairytale lifestyle was over.

Bobby and Linda Brooks became our best friends. Neither Linda nor I worked. Both Bobby and Andrew vowed that their wives would never work outside the home. Even though I was older, Linda was more of a woman of the world. The Brooks had two cars. Linda was bored and she visited me almost everyday. Linda taught me how to use the time-bake function on my oven so that we could prepare the dinner, put it in the oven and have dinner ready when we returned home from our adventure. We would get up in the morning, get the men off to work and the older children off to school, straightened the house, prepared the dinner, put it in the oven on time-bake and hang out together. We got back home just in time for the kids to get off the bus. By the time Andrew came home for dinner, the table was set, the candles were lit, the children were fed, our dinner was ready to be served and I was in a joyous mood.

Linda and I went shopping at least once a week. We usually had lunch while we were out. Like Linda, I ordered a martini with lunch even though I didn't like martinis. I remember the waitress asking if I wanted my martini straight-up or on the rocks. I didn't know what either term meant so I asked for the drink straight-up. I had to sip the drink real slow because I didn't like the taste of the vodka. Linda laughed at me because she knew that I was trying to be something that I was not. She ordered her martini straight-up because she didn't want it to be diluted by the ice.

The more we shopped the weaker our savings accounts became. Even though Linda and I had fun on our days out, we continued to beg our husbands to let us go to work.

I complained about not being able to do the grocery shopping or having to stay home when Andrew was working and using our only car. Andrew bought me a car. Andrew worked ten and twelve hours a day to keep up with the bills. The hours were also a job requirement in the retail industry. Brooks broke down first and let Linda get a job. After Linda started to work Andrew reluctantly let me get a job, on the condition that I kept up with the housework, laundry and cooking.

In early April 1973, I started to work at Aileen's, a sewing factory in Flint Hill, Virginia. I started at minimum wage, $2.10 per hour. Erika and Tony stayed next door with my mother. My family took bets that I wouldn't last two weeks working outside the home because Andrew was very demanding when it came to a clean and orderly house and having his meals on time. It was hard at first. It took a while for me to get my schedule organized to keep up with the requirements of being a working mother. When I got the schedule down pat, I was able to handle all of my work and home responsibilities. Andrew complained that my "little bit of money" messed him up on the taxes. I turned a deaf ear to his complaints because I knew what I had to do.

The more he complained, the harder I worked. The harder I worked the more money I earned. Sewing machine operators were guaranteed to make $2.10 an hour, however the company offered a piece rate incentive. Each bundle of work had a control ticket. When you finished your operation on that bundle you pulled your ticket and the bundle passed on to the next operator. At the end of the day you paste your tickets onto the time sheet.

If your tickets added up to at least $2.10 per hour, you made the rate. If your tickets added up to more than the $2.10 per hour, you beat the rate and you earned that amount of money. I tried different methods to determine which method worked best and reaped the greatest monetary reward. I taped my watch to my sewing machine to time myself and to develop a rhythm. I sat next to the fastest operator performing the same operation as I did. If I focused real hard, I could feel her movements. Every time she picked up a garment, I picked up one too. I tried to keep pace with her, and then I tried beating her time. It wasn't long before I was keeping pace with her and making three, four and five dollars per hour.

One day as I was walking through the office, I saw a board on the wall in the secretary's office. I recognized several of the names on the board. I asked the secretary what was the significance of the board. She said, "Mr. Walker likes to know his top ten operators, this is a list of the top ten operators based on their performance." I wanted my name on the list. I finally got my name on the list. Then I wanted my name on the top of the list.

Once my name was on the list, the plant manager knew me by name and he called me by name. We always had a conversation when we met in the hall. One day as we were walking and talking, I asked Mr. Walker why there weren't any black supervisors in this plant. He responded, "Why do you ask? Do you want to be a supervisor?" I said, "I asked because I wanted to know if I could ever expect to be something more than an operator here at Aileen and no, I don't want to be a supervisor right now. I want to be the number one operator for a year and then I want to work in engineering." He said, "We've had our eyes on someone for supervisor for some time, it just hasn't happened yet." Less than a year later, Aileen's promoted Helen McLee as the first black supervisor.

In 1977, I set a goal to accomplish a solid two-hundred percent productivity for the entire year. I did it. After I accomplished my goal, I made an appointment to go in and talk to Mr. Walker about my future at Aileen. We talked about the possibilities. He tried to make me understand the difference between hourly wages and the salary jobs as it related to the value of the jobs. The engineering position was a salary position and paid less money than I was making on the machine. My productivity with the piece-rate and my performance was not the norm. I had made up my mind to give up the machines and go to the next level. It was hard work maintaining the two-hundred percent productivity level for a year. Most of the other operators hated me and they said, "I was stuck on myself" because I didn't hang out in the bathroom or take breaks in the cafeteria. I used my breaks to put my tickets on my time sheet and organize my work. I had two cousins, Gwen and Cheryl, who also worked at Aileen and we usually had lunch together. Gwen and Cheryl were Fee's children. They were grown now. They didn't put demands on our friendship. I had to focus on the work if I was going to make something of myself.

Mr. Walker was true to his word. He promoted me to Engineering Analyst. The appointment had to be approved by the industrial psychologist. I was sent to the plant psychologist, Dr. LaBryon Mosley. The guys, who had gone through the same routine, came over to me to tell me how proud they were that I was joining their team. They told me what to expect when I met with Dr. Mosley. They told me that Dr. Mosley would ask me to draw myself and I couldn't draw me as a stick person. My appointment was in three days, that wasn't much time. I did not have an ounce of creative ability. I practiced drawing a picture of myself and I was doing pretty good with the practice. When Dr. Mosley handed me the paper and asked me to draw myself and not to draw a stick person, I got so excited I forgot about my practice work and drew what came natural. During the evaluation Dr. Mosley said, "Do you realize that you are hyper?" I told him that, I always had a lot of energy. He said, "You have certainly learned to channel that energy in a positive manner." He said he had heard about my being a two-hundred-percent oper-ator from Mr. Walker. He wanted to know what motivated me to set such a high goal. I said, "My family took bets that I would not work past two weeks because they didn't think that I could handle the pressure of being a working wife and mother. I had to prove that I could not only keep a job but I had to excel in that job. Secondly, I announced to Mr. Walker that I was going to be his number one operator for a year and to do otherwise would have been failure. The fear of failure kept me focused. Besides every time I saw my name at the top of the list I felt good about me. He asked, "What about the money?" I said, "The money was good, however it didn't fit into the equation. It was a factor of trading hours for dollars." Dr. Mosley endorsed me for the management position and I joined the engineering staff as an Engineering Analyst making about a $1,000 less than I was making as a highly productive machine operator.

I knew that to succeed in management would require more education than a high school diploma and strong work ethics. Bubble had graduated from Fisk University, Jimmy had graduated from Cortez Peters Business

School and Patty had graduated from Howard University and even my baby brother, Gene, was attending Howard University. I was the only Kilby child in our family that didn't have any education beyond high school. I felt as though I paved the way for others and in doing so I was cheated out of my own education or was I making an excuse for myself? It was okay because I had come to realize that I wasn't stupid, and I too, could be successful. If I set a goal, made a plan, I could achieve anything through the grace of God.

Late August 1978, I took off work to register my kids in school. As I was going through the newspaper that morning I saw this advertisement in the paper, "Take five classes at Shenandoah College and get a Management Certificate." After I registered the kids in school, I drove to Winchester, Virginia, and registered myself at Shenandoah College for one of the classes listed in the requirements for the Management Certificate. After I filled-out the paperwork and paid my three-hundred-and-seventy-five dollars ($375) for a three-credit course in Organization and Human Behavior I was accepted at Shenandoah College. I was instructed to report to class that following Wednesday evening at seven.

I remembered some fifteen years prior that Daddy had tried to get me into that same college and I wasn't accepted. I didn't say any thing about not being accepted for fear that the school would change their mind and not let me attend the classes. I showed-up that Wednesday for class and sure enough my name was still on the class roster. I was amazed and scared.

I could hardly believe it; my career was on schedule. I had moved into management and now I was in college. Life was good. Good things just don't last long enough. Mr. Walker called me in the office; he complemented me on doing a good job in engineering. I thought I was getting a performance appraisal until he said, "You don't know how much I hate to tell you this but the company lost sales this quarter and I have been instructed to cut indirect labor. The job in engineering has been cut. Because you are such a good operator you will not be laid off. We will also lay off ten percent of our operators but we are going to keep you on as an operator." I was dumbfounded. That night I talked to one of the guys in my class. He said, "We have an opening in Customer Service at Rubbermaid, I know the hiring manager, would you like for me to speak to her for you?" Without hesitation, I said, "Yes." The next day Flo Droll called and scheduled an interview. She offered me the job and I accepted right there on the spot. The pay was about $3,000 less than what I was making at Aileen. Rubbermaid had a tuition-reimbursement policy. It was a larger organization with more career

opportunities. The tuition-reimbursement benefit and the promotion opportunities at Rubbermaid more than compensated for the monetary loss. I
believed that I would move up the corporate ladder quickly because I was
back in school.

It was hard giving my notice to Mr. Walker. I had enjoyed a good working experience at Aileen. Mr. Walker made leaving very difficult because he
was so nice. He told me that I was a remarkable person and that he had not
had an employee that he held in such high regard. He shook my hand,
thanked me for the work that I had performed at Aileen. He said that he was
sorry that I was leaving. Then he just reached out and hugged me. I used
my experience and the effect of the Productivity Board on performance as
my project for my class in, Organization and Human Behavior. Mr. Walker
provided valuable information for the project. He asked if I needed anything
else for the project. I responded, "No, I have just about completed my paper."

I started Rubbermaid on January 15, 1979 as a Customer Service Rep-
resentative. My Rubbermaid anniversary was significant because every year,
I celebrated my anniversary on Dr. Martin Luther King Jr.'s birthday and
it served as a constant reminder of "The Dream." Rubbermaid was quite
different from Aileen. Developing performance credentials was impossible.
Rubbermaid was a more social-driven organization. Very early on, I realized
survival and growth in this company would not be based on what you know,
but, who you know. My friendly personality and liberal attitude enabled me
to talk to everyone from the ladies who cleaned the bathroom to the
executive management staff. I was on a mission to learn as much about
the company and its promotion policy as quickly as possible. Since I had
started as a level three, I was basically on the bottom rung of the ladder and
at the bottom of the pay scale.

When I completed my class in Organization and Human Behavior, I went
in to talk to Flo to find out how I went about getting the tuition reimbursement. Flo told me that I was supposed to fill-out the paperwork prior to
enrolling in the class, but since I accepted the job taking less money, with
the assumption that the pay would be off-set by the tuition reimbursement
she would turn in the fully authorized form along with the copy of my grade.
She also suggested that I should be working toward an Associates Degree at
Lord Fairfax. Lord Fairfax was only twenty-five dollars ($25) per credit
verses the one hundred-and twenty-five dollars ($125) per credit that I was
paying at Shenandoah. I did not tell Flo, but I was afraid that I might not be
accepted into Lord Fairfax because of my high school grades. I applied to

Lord Fairfax anyway and I was accepted. This was even better, now I'm working towards a degree. I went to Daddy and I asked how come Shenandoah College turned me down when I graduated from high school and accepted me this time without questioning my transcript. Daddy said, "Betty, sixteen years have passed, you broke down the barriers, your suffering wasn't in vain."

I was the only African-American employee in Customer Service at that time; therefore most of my close friends and associates were white. Unlike my classmates in high school, most of the people at work were friendly. I seemed to fit in and race didn't appear to matter, except I did not see a single African-American employee in a management position. After six months on the job, I went to Flo and asked her about promotional opportunities. There was a vacancy in our department for a Complaints Coordinator. We discussed the vacancy but I did not perceive our discussion to be an interview. The following week, at our department meeting, Flo announced that Chris Fellars was promoted to Complaints Coordinator. Chris had been with the company longer than me and I was happy for Chris. At Chris's celebration lunch, I sat next to Chris. Chris was a little miffed at me. When I congratulated her, she snapped at me and said, "You come into the department with your bright ideas and now I have to go to Lord Fairfax. I have a family and responsibilities, I don't have time to go to school." I asked, "Can they make you go to school like that?" She looked at me and she said, "You are really naive. None of us in this department have a degree. If you get experience and a degree, you may become the best qualified and they may have to promote you, don't you know anything?"

Chris was Jewish. She told me about how the Ku Klux Klan (KKK) intimidated her family and threatened to burn their house when they lived up North. Her family moved from Ohio because of the KKK. At that point in my life, I thought that the KKK had only threatened blacks and burned homes owned by black citizens. At first I didn't know what to think but I could see the fear in her eyes when she talked about the KKK. I had a warm kindred feeling with Chris because I remembered the Night Riders firing shots at our house. Chris and I became good friends. Generally, we took the same class. Chris taught me how to play the game in Corporate America. She told me who to trust and who to watch.

The department was reorganized and I got the Complaints Coordinator's job in Customer Relations. In the reorganization, this job became a lateral move and I didn't get a raise. My annual raise had brought me up from

$7,500 to $8,600 and I didn't complain about the lateral move. It wasn't a month later a white girl, Dawn Bursey, who had started as a part-time clerk was promoted to a Complaints Coordinator and given a raise. I was irritated by the fact that the person before me and after me was given a raise when coming into the Complaints Coordinator's position, but I didn't say anything because I thought I was being considered for other opportunities. Just after Flo promoted Dawn, she told me that I was being considered for a position in Production, Planning and Inventory Control. She set me up to interview with the manager, Bill Nethers. Right after the interview with Nethers she informed me that Ken Fahnstock, Manager of Engineering was interested in talking to me too.

I was on cloud nine thinking that these people were interested in me and I would be able to choose which job I liked best. It was all smoke and mirrors. The interview in Engineering never materialized. Bill Nethers called me in to tell me that he was impressed with my qualifications, however he felt that I would have been bored in the position. He hired Karen Gallows, a white female, for the position. I knew Karen from Lord Fairfax. She had dropped out of our Financial Management class because she was afraid of failing the class. I was insulted when this white girl was chosen over me. I could see the pattern of discrimination being established.

The guys that worked in the plant were on their break when I arrived for work in the mornings. Every morning they sat at the picnic table in front of the plant entrance and spoke to me when I walked by. After months of passing by these guys, one morning, one of the guys called me over to the table. He stretched forth his hand and said, "Thank you." I asked, "For what?" He said, "Do you realize that we wait here for you every morning? You are the highlight of our day." I said, "No way, I thought this is where you took your break." He said, "The first day we had a bet as to whether you would speak when we spoke to you. We were all surprised when you spoke back." I said, "Please, I was brought up to be polite. Why wouldn't I speak?" The guy who was doing all the talking said, "Because you work in the office." I asked, "What's so special about working in the office? I hear that you guys in the plant make all the money." I looked at my watch and the guy realized that I had to get to work. He said, "You look like you stepped out of *Vogue* magazine, you look and smell so good, you walk so proud and we wanted you to know that we appreciate you." In the days that followed, the number of black guys at the table increased and when I had extra time I would stop and talk.

They also made me take a closer look at the people who worked in the office. I was one of only a handful of African-Americans working in the office.

One Sunday as I was getting ready for church, I fell down the steps and broke the heel on my shoe. It was an expensive pair of shoes. The shoes could not be repaired. Later that week, I went shoe shopping. I realized that expensive shoes were not in the budget. I could only afford to replace the shoes with a cheap pair of shoes. That night I went to class still thinking about those shoes. I met a guy named Mitch Emswiller who also worked at Rubbermaid. Mitch was a second shift supervisor and he worked full time and went to school full time. Mitch poked fun at me. His earnings were three times my earnings and he would have his degree the following year. He said by taking one class per quarter, I would be ready to retire by the time I got my degree. He frowned and said, "You will be forty by the time you graduate." I couldn't sleep that night. I kept thinking about breaking the barriers of education and not getting an education until so late in life. I would get an education so late in life I would always be the unsuccessful Kilby. The next morning I told my husband about my conversation with Mitch. I told him that I wanted to go into the plant and work. Andrew didn't object to my plan. He said, "Do what you want, you always do anyway." Early that morning I spoke with Flo about transferring to the plant. We talked about the money, my inability to get promoted and my conversation with Mitch the night before. She sent me to the Personnel Manager, Bill Baker. Bill reminded me of an old white southern gentleman. I told Bill that I wanted to transfer to the plant and work third shift as a machine operator. Bill said, "Let me talk to you like your Daddy. You know it's dirty down there and that's some hard work. You know that if you go into the plant to work, you can't come back to the office unless you are promoted back." I told him that I was in school. I had done some checking around and determined that if I were working in the plant, I could make more money, take more classes and I could get promoted. He said, "An education alone wouldn't cut it, you need experience and the company only hires experienced people into professional positions." I said, "My Daddy always said that I was stubborn and had to learn the hard way. If I can't get promoted back to the office, I guess I will have to make my career in the plant." I laid the transfer request on his desk, stretched out my hand and said, "I appreciate your candor and concerns, when do you think there will be another opening in the plant?" His expression let me know that he was not happy with my decision to transfer to the plant.

I made it my business to talk to Mitch in class. I told Mitch that I had put in my transfer request for the plant. Mitch arranged for me to take a tour of the plant and watch some of his operators at work. Mitch also informed me that when I came into the plant as an operator he wouldn't be able to show me any special treatment. I responded by, "I don't expect any, but seeing as how I am not an operator yet, can you continue teaching me the ropes?" He smiled and shook his head. A couple weeks later Mitch stopped by my desk to tell me that they had sent a requisition to personnel for two operators. I got a call from personnel informing me of the two open positions on second shift. I thought about second shift in relationship to my family and the classes that I was taking and it wouldn't work. I would have missed too much time with my kids. The company accommodated Mitch's schedule because he was in management. I refused the second shift position. Third shift was the only shift that suited my plan for family and school. A week later, I was called for the third shift vacancy.

After my first night on third shift, I laid on my bed and cried to God, "What have I done? Please give me strength." I drank coffee to keep me awake and it went straight through me. My hands hurt, I had never used power tools before. The boxes were so big and hard to handle. I had trouble even with the simple task of making boxes. The machines and the supplies were up high and I had difficulties reaching both the machine and the supplies. Some of the guys would poke fun at me by saying, "These machines are a lot different from your typewriter, aren't they?" I responded with, "I have a new respect for machine operators." I lost about twenty pounds the first couple of months.

The guys came over to my machine and helped me. They schooled me on the protocol of working in the plant. Each machine had a set of three lights stationed above the machine. The lights were red, yellow and blue. If your machine went down, you turned on the red light signaling that your machine was down and you needed a mechanic. If you needed to talk to a supervisor, you turned on the yellow light and a supervisor came to your machine. The blue light was a call for a material handler who insured that you had boxes, glue, tape or materials. The material handler also operated your machine when you went on break. It was so hard to tell that male material handler, I have to go to the bathroom. Some of the despicable material handlers said things like, "Can't you hold it, didn't you go before you came to work, you need to put a plug in it."

If your machine went down, you were required to help other operators and give them and an extra break. We received two ten-minute breaks and a twenty-minute lunch break.

It took a couple of months to adjust to working in the plant. The boring, repetitive work was the hardest to deal with. I cried every morning for the first month. One morning, I called Andrew at four in the morning crying, "I can't do this." I asked if we could get together for breakfast. We met for breakfast and I was crying before I got into the restaurant. Andrew said, "If you hate it so much, why don't you just quit. I don't understand why you think you have to work, I have always taken care of you." It was just the words I needed to jerk me back to reality. I said, "Quit! Quit! I have never quit anything in my life. I am going to beat this. I need to find the challenge."

The next day I went to work with a new attitude. I went in early and got my assignment. I reported to my machine at least fifteen minutes early. I stripped the old cardboard off the worktable. I put clean cardboard on the table and wrote my class study notes on the table. I developed a rhythm to make the machine operate in the green. I bought a tape recorder. I taped my classes when I was too tired to stay awake in class. I listened to my tapes while I was operating the machines. My grades improved tremendously. I was running even the toughest machine in the green and at last I had adapted to third shift.

I had gradually increased from the one class per quarter to a full-time class load. The first time I enrolled full time, Mr. Baker sent me a note to come by his office before I went home that morning. As a requirement for my degree I had to take a health class. I chose to take Golf. Mr. Baker informed me that some of the classes on my tuition-reimbursement form did not qualify. I said, "I am taking a full-time class load now. If I am reimbursed for the first three classes, the tuition for the entire quarter is covered, the ones that don't qualify are freebies. He looked at the paper and asked, "Can you handle all that and the job too, you know if you don't make at least a "C" you won't get reimbursed. I said, "Yes sir, I am aware, and I can do this."

The guys had a shower in their locker room but there was not a shower in the women's locker room. Before I left Mr. Baker's office, I said, "Mr. Baker, I have a question. Why does the men's locker room have showers and there are no showers in the women's locker room." He said, "The mechanics get dirty and greasy working on the machines and the showers were primarily for the mechanics. Since there were no female mechanics at the time the showers were installed in the men's locker rooms, we didn't put showers in the women's locker room." I said, "We have one female mechanic now and I would like to have an opportunity to shower before I go to class. One of the guys that I work with is not a mechanic and he told me that he showers before he goes to class. The most that I can do is freshen up. What is the possibility of getting a shower in the women's locker room?" Within two months there was a shower in the women's locker room. When the company put showers in the women's locker rooms, I got the respect from my fellow female operators because they instinctively knew that I had raised the issue.

The following quarter at Lord Fairfax College as I put together my class schedule, I had sufficient credits to get a Certificate in Supervision. My advisor suggested that I sign-up for the Cooperative Education Program. I signed up but my supervisor refused to approve the program because it had not been done before in the plant among the other operators. There were people in the office and management working at Rubbermaid and participating in the program. My advisor called my supervisor to try to explain the program to him but he was not able to change my supervisor's mind. I had to drop the class.

I made an appointment with Mr. Baker. I informed him that I had completed the requirements for a Certificate in Supervision and that I was interested in a supervisor's position. It wasn't long before I saw the announcement that another one of the white guys was promoted to supervisor. I made another appointment with Mr. Baker, this time I wanted to know what was the process to be considered for a vacancy for supervisor. He said that he made the determination along with the plant manager who would interview the candidates for a supervisor's position when a vacancy occurred. I said, "Sixty percent of the operators are female and there are no female supervisors. I have a Certificate in Supervision as well as an Associates Degree. I think I would make a good supervisor. I am ready to use the education paid for by the company." He reminded me that he told me before that just because I got an education didn't mean that I was qualified to be anything because I didn't have any experience. I said, "As I think about conversations with the last two supervisors promoted, all they had was experience as operators, no prior supervisory experience and no education beyond high school." I pulled copies of the recent promotion announcements from my folder and handed them to Mr. Baker. I had written the following note on each announcement, "no college, no prior experience." Bill replied, "We will see."

A month later, I received a letter informing me that I had been scheduled along with several other candidates to take a battery of tests and interviews for a supervisor's position. My mind went back to the stories of colored people and their efforts in getting the right to vote and the stupid test that they were required to take. I asked some of the other supervisors about the process that they went through to get their supervisor jobs. None of them were required to take a test.

There were about fifteen people taking the test. I was the only African-American candidate, there were two white female candidates and the rest were white male candidates. I was not surprised that there were no other African-American employees being considered since we had an African-American male supervisor in the plant. I worked with one of the females (Jeannie Shobe) in the plant, the other female (Jane Saville) worked in the shipping office and she had been with the company less than six months. I asked my friend in shipping about her and he said she wasn't too bright. After the test, I had an opportunity to talk to one of the white guys, Jim Green. Jim said that one part of the test was the same as the Material Handlers test that he had taken previously.

George Hill and associates administered the test. When the results of the test came in, the Hill consultant sat down with me to review my scores. I scored in the eighty to ninety percentiles as compared to most managers taking the test in every area except the technical area. The Hill consultant was intrigued by the fact that the more complicated and higher level math problems I was able to master but I missed some less complicated problems. He picked out a couple of examples to review. I asked, "What grade level would an individual have to have to solve this type of problem?" The math problems that I missed were math skills that I would have learned in high school. I explained that my high school experience was a hellish experience, I had recently received my Associates Degree and that I was presently working towards my Bachelor's Degree.

About a month after the testing, the company announced that Jim Proffit, Charlie Burnett and Paul Simmons had been promoted to a newly created position, Technical Supervisor. A Technical Supervisor was named for each shift and the mechanics would report to the Technical Supervisor instead of the shift supervisor. I was encouraged, if I scored high in every section except the technical, with the implementation of technical supervisors, technical skills shouldn't rank as high in the requirements for the shift supervisor.

About two months after the testing, the shift manager, John Kirkham, informed me that I made the short list. The five candidates were given two days to prepare a one-page paper presenting a case where each of us demonstrated problem solving skills, person-to-person skills, mechanical ability, planning and priority setting, organizational skills and decision-making skills. After the papers were reviewed, John Kirkham and Plant Managers, Craig Sullivan, Jack Mueller and Bill Walthers; and the Personnel Manager Bill Baker interviewed each of us. The position reported to Craig Sullivan. Two days after the interview, I was called in and informed that Jane Saville had been selected. I was told that I wasn't selected because of my low technical scores. I rose from my chair, stretched forth my hand and thanked John Kirkham for the opportunity to interview for this position and left his office.

I went straight to the ladies room, locked myself in a stall, got down on my knees and talked to God until I could talk about not getting the job without an emotional outburst. I knew that someone would ask about my reaction to Jane's selection as shift supervisor and I needed to be prepared to react appropriately.

The days and weeks that followed were almost unbearable. Everyone was shocked over Jane's promotion. Most of the people thought, if the intent were to hire a white woman, Jeannie Shobe would have been selected over Jane because Jeannie was in the Supervisory Development Program. My peers in the plant expected me to fight because they believed that African-Americans were systematically being discriminated against and I could not disagree. I didn't want to fight because it would be like Warren County all over again, never a moment of peace. These kinds of battles you fight with your soul. My white friends in Customer Service wanted to know how long was I going to make everyone else go to school so that management could keep me out. They were saying that the company had become so bold as to bring Jane in from the outside, train her on the test so that she could score high, just to keep this one little colored girl out. A couple of the girls in Customer Service volunteered to testify that Jane received extra training. They complained that she could not get her regular job done because she was always in training. Jane's job position provided shipping support for the Customer Service department.

I was put in the Supervisory Development Program. One of my black brothers said, "Give the Nigger a crumb and she is satisfied." I got defensive and asked, "What have you done to improve the situation for our people?"

He said that he was trying to get the Union representation. I said, "My Dad belonged to the Union but the white Union leadership didn't do squat except take his Union dues. It is management that will ultimately make a difference and impact change." He said, "Well, make yourself satisfied in the Supervisory Development Program because you will be there for as long as Ron Nelson is supervisor, they only need one little Nigger in management to make the numbers." I walked away but his words stayed in my head.

One morning, I looked in the mirror and I asked God how many cheeks did I have left to turn. One of my white friends was a minister. I walked up to him at his machine and I said, "Put your hand on my shoulder and act as though you are talking to me, but I want you to pray for me in this unholy place as I go to apply for another management position in the office." He prayed for me. We touched and agreed in the name of Jesus that His will be done. I went up to personnel to talk to Mr. Baker. I had heard that Flo Droll had announced her retirement. Mr. Baker invited me into his office and shut the door. He said, "Well what do you want this time? How many ways do we have to tell you? You are never going to get anywhere around here because you don't have any experience and you won't ever get any experience." I got up without uttering a word. All the way home, I asked, "God, why me? I don't want to fight. Is that my purpose here on earth?" I begged "Please don't make me do this." When I got home I went to my file, pulled out the calendar and counted the days since Jane's promotion — all the while begging God to not make me do this. Fifty-eight days. I took my shower and got dressed. I drove to Richmond to the Equal Employment Opportunity Commission (EEOC). I made it to Richmond in less than two hours arguing with God all the way. Having worked with the NAACP, I knew about discrimination and the process for filing a charge. I stated only the facts. Who? What? When? Where? I knew better than to talk about the conversation with Mr. Baker, I couldn't believe that he said what he did, so how could I tell anyone else?

When I came out of the EEOC it was four in the evening. The parking had expired and the tow truck was hooking the tow bar to my car. I fell across my car crying out, "Why God, why God, Whhhyyyy? Please don't take my car." The man detached the tow bar from my car. He must have thought I was stone crazy. I got home in time to take another shower, spend a little time updating Andrew and going back to work.

Working full time, going to school full time, I learned the value of the power nap. I could lay on the bench in the locker room, set my watch alarm, sleep ten or twenty minutes and function for the rest of the night. I had to play by the rules. I could not get caught sleeping on the job or not performing to the highest standard.

I was in training in the Supervisor Development Program working for Jim Hosteller in the Quality Control department. Jim was pretty cool. Every morning I would update Jim on what went on during the third shift. Occasionally, I made suggestions of ways to improve the operation in Quality Control. One morning after Jim realized that I had taken the initiative to read the "Quality Control Training Manual" Jim confessed, "At one point I thought you were involved in Union activity; I am so glad that I had an opportunity to get to know the real you." The company didn't have a Union. There was Union activity and I knew some of the key players. Some of the operators were soliciting other operators to sign cards to have a vote. I told Jim how the Union treated my Daddy during integration — and bottom line — I wanted to be in management. I believed that management could do more to make the workplace better. He said that he watched the attitude of my peers towards me when Jane Saville became supervisor and he realized that he was wrong in his assumptions about me. He wrote a glowing review concerning my performance.

A couple of weeks later, Ron Nelson, the only African-American supervisor and my supervisor at the time asked me to take a walk with him to the warehouse. As we walked he said, "You just couldn't leave it alone could you? You make things harder for yourself." I said, "I wish I could have left it alone but I couldn't." He said, "I have been instructed to put you back on the machine." I said, "No problem." He said, "Well, let's go back in the office and I will thank you for the good job that you did in QA and I will tell you that there are no more training opportunities at this time. I will also talk to Jeannie Shobe." We went to Ron's office and Ron did his job. The same time that I went back on the machine as an operator; so did Jeannie. Jeannie dropped her head when she approached me and I knew she blamed me for the termination of the program.

Things got so bad that I went to talk to my Daddy. I asked Daddy how did he take the daily harassment at work during integration? Daddy said, "The first thing you have to do is determine why you are fighting. I could never have taken all the abuse if I were fighting for a promotion, money or myself. I was fighting for you, Jimmy, Bubble, Pat and Gene. I knew that someday you would be working and I had hoped that you would not have to be fighting for that economic prosperity we talked about during integration. I had hoped that jobs and promotions would be easy for you once you got an education. I guess our time hasn't come yet. Second, evaluate the consequences of your actions and turn the tables. When I get into the damn if you do, and damn if you don't, situations I will piss off my opponent. You know when your opponent gets mad they don't think straight. Lastly, I prayed all the time and I listened to God. When I was scared out of my mind and my heart beat so fast I thought it was going to pop through my skin, I found a quiet place like in the stairwell and meditated until I felt the calmness of God." I got up to leave and Daddy said, "I'm real proud of the way that you came through integration and everything." I hugged him and skipped back to my house next door.

I knew that had I left things alone and had I not filed the EEO charge against the company, I would eventually have become supervisor. I had not filed the charge for a promotion. Some of the company leadership systematically controlled the promotions to limit the promotions of African-Americans in the company. My peers in the plant and in Customer Service also knew that the company had discriminated against me. There was no way that I could allow Mr. Baker to talk down to me as he did. If I stood by and did nothing, I would give him the power to believe that he could hold back a whole race of people by separating us and saying anything he pleased in the privacy of his office, where it would be my word against his. Who would people believe? A company official in his right mind would have more sense than to say such things to an employee. This was the scariest situation that I had been in since high school. Daddy had given me a lot to think about. The one thing I was sure of was, the fight was not about my own selfish gain.

I kept applying for jobs and I kept getting turned down. Jennie Shobe, became the second white female supervisor in the plant. I had dropped out of college because my daughter Erika had been diagnosed as a diabetic. We were having difficulties adjusting to the morning doctor appointments and the spiking of her sugar levels. I was being forced to work overtime because I was at the bottom of the overtime list. I called in sick after spending all day at the hospital with Erika on a couple of occasions and I was too close to violating the total number of absences allowed.

On February 17, 1984, John Kirkham counseled me on my attendance. I was asked to sign a statement that I understood that I would not be promoted during the year. I refused to sign the document. I said, "I will sign any document acknowledging that this was my fifth occurrence of being absent. I will comment on my past years with perfect attendance because I have not abused the absentee policy. I will comment on my daughter's health. I will state the facts surrounding the fifth occurrence since I had food poisoning and I was taken from here to the hospital in the ambulance." During this time, the company promoted Jeannie and slapped me with the first and only infraction — without any concern for my past performance.

The next day, I hired a lawyer and my lawyer had the EEO case transferred to the Washington, D.C. EEOC office. Approximately one year after I had filed the charge, the EEOC began its investigation. When my paid attorney began requesting documents, I was put back in the Supervisor Development Program. I was assigned acting supervisor on third shift for six weeks. When that assignment was complete, I was assigned to first shift as acting supervisor for another six weeks. Mr. Baker retired.

I knew that I was assigned to first shift so that I could be evaluated I invested in some new work clothes. Dress suits were not appropriate attire for a supervisor in the plant, therefore I purchased loose-fitting skirts that came to the calf of my legs. I purchased a good pair of one-inch wedge heel shoes. The first morning that I reported to work wearing a skirt, John Kirkham asked, "Is that appropriate attire? We have never had a woman to wear a dress in the plant before." I answered, "I checked the employee manual and it is not specific on dress code except for shoes and the only specifications is no sandals." John said, "You look very nice and it's a refreshing look."

I was the only woman in the morning meeting. The guys started the meeting with a joke. Most of the jokes were awful and in such poor taste that I could not condone them. I kept a straight face without smiling even at the clean and funny jokes. I did not participate in any of the jokes. One morning one of the guys told a funny joke and I never cracked a smile. He singled me out and asked "What's wrong with you?" I looked him straight in the eye and said, "I don't participate in jokes of any kind because you start with funny, work through the ethnic jokes and eventually you start cracking on my people and I'll have to knock the living shit out of you." The words slipped out of my mouth with out my thinking. You could have heard a pin fall in the meeting. John Kirkham said, "Shall we continue with the meeting?" Later that day, John came over and said, "I am glad that you responded to the joke this morning. What is living shit?" I chuckled and said, "It's an expression that I heard the old folks say when you were about to get a whipping." At the meeting the next morning John jumped right in with the business. One of the guys told me that John had talked to each of the participants in the morning meeting and had informed each one that out of respect for the fact that there was a lady in the meeting the jokes would be discontinued and the language would be cleaned up. If one of the guys slipped and used unacceptable language, they would apologize to me personally. I always responded with, "Apology accepted."

The assignment was challenging but I enjoyed every challenge because each time that I responded appropriately I gained a little bit more respect. One day, one of the mechanics waited until my operator went to lunch and started one of the machines in my section. I had been bugging him to get the machine up and running. He said the machine would not be up and running for over an hour. Right after I sent the operator on break, I noticed the light on. I went over to the machine and said, "I thought it was going to take an hour to get this machine up and running." He said, "Woman, you kept bugging me about this machine, now it's running, do you want me to shut it down?" I said, "Oh no, I got it, thank you for getting this machine going for me." He said, "You don't have an operator." I said, "I got it." I ran the machine and the operator promptly returned from his lunch break.

The last thing that I had to do for my evaluation was to have a staff meeting. It could not be a mandatory meeting and I was going to be graded based on the number of employees that attended the early morning meeting. I sat in the office thinking about who would show up and who would not show up. I thought about the various conversations with my work group. That night when I went home, I sat down and wrote each one of the employees a personal invitation to the staff meeting. At the end of the note I wrote, "coffee and doughnuts will be served." I even wrote an invitation to my supervisor (Bill Walthers) who would be evaluating my performance. I asked if the company would pick up the tab for the coffee and doughnuts. He looked at me half smiling and with somewhat of a puzzled look and asked, "Where do you come up with such ideas?" I responded by saying, "These guys are always talking about how the people in the office have doughnuts and coffee at their meetings and they want to be treated with the same respect as the office employees. I try to treat them with the utmost respect." The morning of the meeting, all of my staff had showed up except for one person, Shakey. He was a difficult employee and I was constantly watching him. He would leave his workstation when his machine went down and relieve the person who worked in the tool shed. Most of the operators didn't like Shakey because he was not perceived as a team player. He rarely helped his fellow operators when his machine went down. Having observed how much pride Shakey put in straightening out the tool shed, I assigned Shakey to the tool shed every chance I got. Five minutes into the meeting, Shakey walks in with sausage biscuits and homemade jelly. He said, "My wife wanted to make your last day on first shift special." I had never met his wife. He sat the basket on the table, pulled back the towel, reached in, got a biscuit and said, "Eat up they are still warm." The room began to smell like Grandma's kitchen. I was a little fearful, I quickly asked God to forgive me for all my sins, to go with and stand by me as I reached in, got a sausage biscuit and passed the basket to Bill Walthers. I was so excited that I could hardly conduct the meeting. Many of the guys hugged me as they left the meeting.

I dreaded going back to third shift as a machine operator. I intensified my search for a permanent management position. I saw the vacancy announcement on the bulletin board for a Scheduler. I talked to my supervisor, Bill Walthers. Bill said he would talk to the hiring manager, Dallas Norris, on my behalf. Less than two weeks later I went to third shift as a back-up supervisor. I discovered that a white male, Don Strosnider was going to work on a temporary assignment as a Scheduler. I was so ticked-off I could hardly think straight. During my lunch break, I sat in the car and listened to my favorite song, "I'm Coming Up on the Rough Side of the Mountain." When Bill came in that morning as I was getting off work, I asked if I could talk to him. He asked if I would like to go to his office. I said, "No, I am so mad that I would prefer to walk and talk to maintain my composure.

I asked, "What is it going to take for me to get promoted around here? I have succeeded in every assignment that you have given me with excellent performance reviews, I've given 120% in every assignment but every time an opportunity is available, you promote one of your boys. You send me back to third shift while you send Don Strosnider to work for Dallas after you promised that you would talk to Dallas Norris on my behalf. I thought you were a man of your word." He said, "Dallas needed someone fast and Don was the first to come to mind." I said, "Yea right, thanks for nothing."

The next morning I received an invitation to meet with the new Human Resource Manager, Bob Henningsen. Bob was conducting individual, getting-to-know-you meetings with the non-management employees. I didn't know what to expect, therefore I wanted to be prepared. I went to get my Rubbermaid folder. Amazing, like my Daddy, I kept my papers in the car under the seat. Documents were coded with colored paper clips. I reviewed the documents in the file, just in case, I needed to refer to a document. The largest stack were the copies of job descriptions of the positions that I had applied for and didn't get during my time at Rubbermaid. The "getting-to-know-you" session was scheduled for an hour, however, it lasted two hours. Bob had my official personnel file on his desk. I was intrigued. I asked, "May I?" Bob said, "Let's review it together." We went through my personnel file, tuition reimbursement, training, performance reviews and attaboy letters. They were all good. We went through my attendance record, all good except one. I explained Erika's health problems. We went through my test results and recommendations. Bob asked, "What do you think of the promotional opportunities here at Rubbermaid?" I pulled the stack of jobs that I had applied for and didn't get. I said, "Over the past five years, I have applied, interviewed and was turned down twenty-three times. I went to school, earned a Certificate in Supervision and an Associates Degree in Business Management, and not a single promotion. I have not seen a single African-American promoted to a management position in the past five years. There are tremendous opportunities if you are a white man or white woman here at Rubbermaid. I even told him about the EEO claim.

Two days after my meeting with Bob Henningsen, I was called to schedule an interview for the Scheduler's position with Dallas Norris. I interviewed. Seven days later, I was offered the job. On October 29, 1984, I started to work in the office as a Scheduler. I had accomplished something that most people had deemed impossible.

Jackson, the guy who had sat at the picnic table and took bets as to whether I would speak came up to me during my promotion celebration and said, "Well, are you going to speak to us when you go back to the office?" I responded, "Please, I was brought up to be polite. Why wouldn't I speak?" We both laughed. I stretched forth my hand to say thank you. Jackson said, "Don't give me your hand, you are my hero and I want a hug." I hugged him and I said, "I truly want to thank you for your support. There were days when I first started in the plant that I went home in tears. It was all I could do to keep from quitting, your encouragement kept me coming back. Whether you realize it or not you are a leader amongst the operators. They echoed your encouragement and all of you taught me how to fit in as an operator.

At the lowest ebb in my life when my overtime got low you guys jumped in and worked for me. Everything that I have accomplished was because you and all the guys that look up to you were there for me."

My white friend who had prayed with me came up and hugged me, and confessed, "When I first met you I was intimidated by you. You walk and talk so proud, you vowed that you were going to get promoted back to the office and I thought that was pride. I thought you didn't care when you were so calm and confident. The day you started wearing dresses, I thought 'She doesn't belong in the plant.' Then, that day you asked me to pray with you, I realized how truly special you are. God put you here to touch our lives; He set you apart so that He could show us how wrong we were to judge you. You have blessed me." The outpouring of love and accolades from both my peers and superiors balanced the scale of joy and pain.

My first day in scheduling, I had an abscessed tooth. One whole side of my face was swollen. I called my dentist and scheduled an afternoon appointment. I went to work. I had to report to Dallas's office. He took one look at me and said, "You should not have come in this morning. I saw the write up and the perfect attendance letters in your personnel file and we are not as strict as the plant." I informed him that I had a dentist appointment that afternoon. Dallas said, "If your face is still swollen tomorrow, you call me and stay home." The next day I called in and told Dallas that I needed to have a root canal but I had to wait until after the abscess healed.

On the third day Dallas gave me a training schedule. The department was scheduled for a team-building session to be held the following weekend in Arlington, Virginia. The people from the scheduling departments in Cleburne, Texas, and Centerville, Iowa, would also be a part of this team-building training. To cut expenses, we were asked to share rooms. I was the only African-American in the department, therefore, my roommate would be a white female; a white female that I didn't know. I was really uncomfortable and I dreaded this training. I thought about every aspect of having to share the room with a white girl. As I thought about having to share the bathroom, I thought about the difference in our hair. If it were my white friend Vickie, it would have been fine, I would have just said, "Look Vickie, my hair is not like yours when it gets wet, here's the deal." My daughter Renée had what we called the "white-people's hair." I had to take her to the white beautician to figure out how to do her hair. She washed her hair everyday, white people tend to think people who don't wash their hair everyday are dirty. Would my roommate think I was dirty if I didn't wash my hair every day? There was that old myth that black people stink, what would she think? After much deliberation, I had my hair cut to shorten the time it would take to curl it in the morning with the curling iron. I kept a perm in my hair so even if it got wet, it wouldn't be a major problem. Dallas asked that we bring family pictures.

As I packed, I carefully chose clothes that made me feel good about me. I sat in front of the mirror and looked myself straight in the eye and said, "You probably paid a greater price to be in that training than anyone there, you have earned the right to be there. You are a child of God full of grace and beauty, if God be for you, who shall be against you." As usual I was the first one in the office that morning. As the others came in, I was poised, confident and ready. That night at dinner as we showed off our pictures, I knew they were dying to ask about "my rose garden family." Finally, my Texas roommate, Lawanna, felt comfortable enough to ask. As I explained my "kitchen baby" concept, everyone got very quiet. Finally, I said, "You do know the history of America don't you?" Later when we went back to the room Lawanna wanted to know more about being black. She commented that black people have better advantages because of the Civil Rights Act. I reared back in the chair and I said, "Girl, what hole have you had your head buried in? Before I could think, I had told her about the whole ordeal in the plant, Jane Saville, the EEO charge, high school. I stopped short of telling her about being raped because the tears swelled up in my eyes and the pain brought me to silence. She said, "I am sorry." I thought about my conversation to myself that morning, gained my composure and said, "Don't be sorry, learn about other people, never make assumptions and believe only half of what you hear." I asked, "You already knew about the EEO charges didn't you?" She said, "Yes, my boss Diane told me about it. But I didn't know about your high school experience, you filled in the blanks because I had questions." Diane was Dallas's counterpart in the Texas office. While we were in the midst of a sensitive discussion, I thought it was time to discuss the bathroom and the hair. I asked Lawanna if she wanted to use the bathroom first. She said she wasn't a morning person. I was a morning person. I got up the next morning, took my shower, did my hair and woke up Lawanna after I was dressed.

An outside consulting firm facilitated the meeting. During the meeting we developed our job description, job standards and performance standards. I told the group about my experience with the piece rate at Aileen and how

I believed in performance standards. We had to discuss our career plans. I talked about having dropped out of school when my daughter Erika became a diabetic. I promised the group that I would go back to school and finish the requirements for my bachelor's degree. The group promised to be there to encourage me to complete my goal. I told Dallas that I was just a little apprehensive about the meeting but I thought the idea of team building was brilliant.

I learned a lot about the job. The exercise in developing the job description, job standards and performance standards enabled me to meet and exceed my every expectation.

My immediate supervisor, Ken Fahnstock, left the company. Craig Sullivan was promoted to take over as Scheduling Manager. Craig was the hiring manager who hired Jane Saville over me. He was specifically named in the EEO case. Craig had not spoken to me since he got the news of the case and he was the only section manager that did not congratulate me when I was promoted into scheduling. I was frightened over the possibility of working for this man. I dreaded what I had determined to be the 1,001 things that a manager could do to set you up and break you. Because he refused to speak to me, I didn't trust him.

A couple of weeks after Craig became my supervisor, Dallas called me into his office. When I sat down he said he called me in because he was concerned about my performance. I asked, "Can you excuse me a minute please?" I walked to my car. I was like a bull seeing red. All the way to the car, I kept saying, "Calm down, calm down," I heard Daddy saying in the background, "If you are mad you make mistakes, you don't think." I got my performance folder from the car.

When I got back in the building, I stopped by the ladies room, got down on my knees in the stall and silently prayed that God guide my tongue, hold back the tears and I asked that He speak for me. I went back to Dallas's office, opened my folder and asked, "Dallas, show me what area my performance has slipped, how much and what do I need to do to correct it." My voice changed and I was so composed that it scared me. Dallas was quiet for so long, I said, "Talk to me." He said, "You don't smile like you used to, you are not as friendly as you use to be." I said, "Dallas, in the team-building meeting we promised to be honest with each other, I am going to be real honest with you and I am praying that you will be honest with me. This conversation is not about my performance. You and I both know it's about Craig. Every week I evaluate my performance. Here is the graph for the past two months, it shows improvement rather than a dip in my performance. Craig treats me as if I don't exist. He goes through the motions. I have survived because I trust when my heart says I can trust. I have put up my guard. I am a soldier trained in the war of wills. I have been a soldier since I was thirteen fighting for an education. You see, when we integrated the schools, my father told us over and over again that we were in a war to get an education. Our opponents were determined to keep us from getting an education and keeping us from achieving this level of success. That war is still on. It is my desire to achieve the highest level of any white individual with the same education and experience. My blackness will not hold me back without a fight. There is no degree of hurt, harm or danger — that I haven't already experienced and survived — that can keep me from achieving the highest degree of performance and from expecting upper mobility and professional growth." Sometime during the conversation, I must have stood up. I turned toward the door when Dallas said, "Please wait, I apologize, I have misjudged you, please forgive me." I stretched forth my hand and said, "Apology accepted, I am tired of fighting. I simply want to live an honest and honorable life, do my job and be evaluated fairly."

I focused on doing a good job. I carefully evaluated my every move, choosing my words and battles carefully. I drew from all of my experiences to meet and exceed performance standards. I did not go back to school because I had to be focused on the job. I changed the economic manufacturing quantities (EMQ) drew a decision tree and performed "what if" analysis. I prayed over my decisions. When Craig questioned my decision to reduce the manufacturing quantities, I was smooth in answering his questions. I spoke with such authority that Craig was impressed. When I lowered the inventory and maintained service levels, he acknowledged my performance, however, I never let down my guard.

Craig was promoted after about six months. Dick Helsley became the scheduling manager. I felt comfortable working for Dick and I was able to relax. I had built a solid knowledge base of the job and I believed I could perform this job with both eyes closed.

In September 1985, I decided it was time to complete the requirements for my B.S. degree. I went to my advisor at Shenandoah College to see what I needed to graduate. I needed twenty-two credits. My advisor, Dr. Denis Driscole, advised that it was impossible to complete the requirements for graduation in one semester, by May of 1986. I needed a science credit. I took Chemistry for the first half of my science requirement. I passed with a "C".

I got the "C" because I latched on to a first year student like a leech. She was fresh out of high school, she was good at chemistry and she agreed to be my lab partner. We made an "A" on the lab work.

In analyzing my plan for graduation, I decided to take Geology at Lord Fairfax Community College to fulfill my science requirement and take a full class load at Shenandoah College. I reviewed my plans with my supervisor, Dick Helsley. Dick agreed to let me enroll in the Work Study Program that would give me three easy credits.

I began to move up in the department very rapidly without asking or fighting. I went from Scheduler to Senior Scheduler and to Supervisor of Inventory Management. Just when I thought it would be a good year, I was scheduled to meet with the EEOC, my lawyer and Rubbermaid's Vice President of Human Resources, Robert Henningsen (Bob). My heart pounded with excitement. I went shopping for a new suit. I found a dark purple suit, single-breasted with a short jacket. The meeting was at the EEO office in Washington, D.C. At the meeting Bob agreed to everything that I had asked for in October 1983. I did not argue any of the points since I was getting everything I asked for and I was paying my lawyer by the hour. When the company agreed to promote me to Production Supervisor, Grade 18, I had already achieved Grade 18 and the last thing I wanted to do was go back to the plant as a second or third shift supervisor. The EEOC drew up the papers and sent them to Rubbermaid.

On February 11, 1986, I got a call from Bob's secretary asking me to come to Bob's office. When I arrived in Bob's office and sat down, Bob handed me the "Negotiated Settlement Agreement." I reminded Bob that I was already at a Grade 18, and I was happy working in Scheduling, he said that he would work with me. When I read paragraph (4) "It is understood that this Agreement does not constitute an admission by the Respondent of any violation of Title VII of the Civil Rights Act of 1964, as amended or any other applicable state or federal statute or any action at common law. This Agreement does not constitute a contract of employment nor alter the employment-at-will relationship between Respondent and Charging Party." My spirit dropped to an all time low. I said, "Two years of hell all in vain." Bob said, "Standing up for something that you believe in is never in vain." As hard as I tried I could not fight back the tears. I was overcome with emotion. Bob handed me a pen and I signed the agreement. He handed me a check for four thousand, thirty-one dollars and ninety-three cents ($4,031.93), the difference between my rate of pay from October 1983 through November 1985 and that of Jane Saville for the same period.

I got my BS degree in Business Administration in May of 1986. Rubbermaid hired its first African-American Engineer Grade 21. He was young and well-qualified for the job. He barely spoke and had no time to associate with anyone except his work group. This was not unnatural or unexpected because most of the Engineers were set-off from most of the other employees. He was a safe hire. He most likely would not be making waves and was mostly interested in Engineering. I silently felt a sense of accomplishment. While they did not admit to any discrimination, they did hire an African American into a mid-level management position.

Andrew's father died suddenly of a massive heart attack leaving Andrew's mother bed-ridden and alone. It was my selfish desire to marry an only child, however in the difficult days following Andrew's fathers death, I wished that he had brothers and sisters to help with his mother. After a couple of years of commuting from Front Royal to Middleburg to cut grass, grocery shop, hire housekeepers, we realized a nursing home was inevitable. I did the necessary research. Upon completion of my research, I coined the phrase, "You come into this world with nothing and you will leave this world with nothing. All that we have are the things that we see and do while we are here." Andrew's mother was sucking the life out of us. We had to do something. I was back in school working on my MBA. My husband and I discussed the situation. We decided that since I was working on my MBA, I should quit my job to take care of her affairs. It would be easier for me to get back into the workforce after I got my MBA.

We hired housekeepers and she fired them. On one occasion when his mother fired the housekeeper, she fell and broke her hip. The authorities told Andrew that he could not leave her in the house alone. Despite the fact that she violently objected to the nursing home, we had no choice but to admit her. She was moved from the hospital to the nursing home in an ambulance and she thought she was still in the hospital until one of the neighbors visited her and let it slip that she was in a nursing home. She got so mad she had to be sedated.

My mother-in-law gave my husband Power-of-Attorney shortly after his father died. It enabled us to liquidate her estate easily and quickly. Should my mother-in-law outlive her assets, my husband would be called upon to justify her financial status, therefore, we had to make sure that her estate was liquidated in a manner that could be documented. I contacted an auctioneer to handle the sale of her personal effects. He asked if we planned to auction off the house. The thought had not crossed my mind. I asked, "How do you make sure that you get fair market value when you auction the house?" He said, "With a minimum bid." I told him that I had to consult with my husband. My husband decided that it was a good idea. I put the auction advertisement in the local newspapers, made flyers and distributed throughout the community. A lot of family and friends came to the auction. My in-laws were well-respected in the community. I was upset over having to sell my in-law's personal effects until a friend and family member expressed happiness about having an opportunity to purchase something that was once owned by someone they cared about. The house was also sold that day to a distant relative.

When I gave my notice, Dallas suggested that I take a leave of absence rather than quit. He offered to work with me until the situation improved. I was shocked when Bob Henningsen came over and expressed his willingness to work with alternatives to quitting. I gave serious considerations to taking the leave rather than quitting.

It was two years since my case was settled. I was back in school working on my MBA because there seemed to be no way to get to the next level. I could not develop that level of trust that I perceived to be absolutely necessary in achieving the levels that I had set for myself. I believed that I would be able to write my own ticket with experience at mid-level management and an MBA. I wanted to know what it would feel like to work in an organization that wanted me for my skills and the abilities that I brought to the table. I wanted to know what it would be like to be in school without the pressures of work, to have plenty of time to work on a project. I decided to quit, pay the penalty, take my retirement money and have the time of my life.

I did not tell my employer the total extent of the problems that I was dealing with. My Mother had a heart attack in December. Even though we lived next door to each other, we were not close. I had old baggage and I needed to make amends with my Mother and improve our relationship.

My third daughter, Erika, was pregnant out of wedlock by a white boy who was facing twenty years in prison for his involvement in a ring of thieves. He robbed local businesses to support his drug addiction. He even robbed my daughter's place of work and put her in legal jeopardy.

Times had changed since my disgrace of being pregnant out of wedlock. Even though times had changed I had a very difficult time dealing with my daughter's pregnancy. It was my past sins jumping up and smacking me in my face. I had asked for God's forgiveness and I was forgiven. I had barely gotten over the empty nest syndrome. I thought I was much to young to be a grandmother. When my first grandson, Eric, arrived on May 4, 1989, he was beautiful and the joy of my life.

Not working a full-time job allowed me to stretch my wings. The only black member on the Town Council was not going to run for another term. A committee of black citizens was looking for a black candidate to run. They approached me. My very first response was "Hell no." One of the guys approached me again. He stroked my ego by telling me how much the community needed a good African-American leader. After our discussion, I decided to run for the seat on the Town Council. It was a three-way race.

My life became an open book. It opened up a lot of old wounds that many local people harbored from the integration days. I was accused of serving my Father's agenda. Over the years, my Daddy never let up. He said during integration that it was about economic empowerment. His name or picture was always in the newspaper. He was such a warrior, fighting for the rights and privileges of our people. More often than not he was successful. Whether it was getting low- and moderate-income people get in houses, helping people to resolve issues on the job or at school, or helping people to get out of jail; there was Daddy. Local folks feared, KILBY.

People working on my campaign told me that I had to distance myself from my Daddy. I had come to love and respect the man so much and there was no way that I could deny my birthright. Some of my supporters refused to work on my campaign after I refused to distance myself from my Daddy. I hadn't thought about the impact of my running for political office on my family. I thought because my last name was Fisher and my children's last name was Fisher they would not have been penalized because of me. Wrong!

The traditional method of campaigning was the door-to-door campaign. The door-to-door campaign was fun. Some people were waiting for me to come to their door. I could talk to anybody. We ran a lean and mean campaign. Most of my donations came in the form of cash. Some of the white folks would roll up $20 and put it my hand and say, "Buy some advertising." Our strategy was to buy posters early in the campaign and do a blitz two weeks before the election. I knew that many people respected me but they feared supporting me publicly.

The morning after the election the headlines in one of the local news-papers read, "Kitts and Miller wins, Fisher loses." I lost the race by three votes. I had mixed emotions about losing the election. Having lost by only three votes, I could have requested a recount. I told the news reporters that I would come back in two years and run for Mayor. I did run for Mayor in two years and lost by a much greater margin.

My Mother and I became friends, as well as mother and daughter. On one occasion when I was negotiating the sale of the house that we purchased while my daughters were in college, my Mother dressed-up in her business suit and attended the meeting with me. On the way home from the meeting she laughed and talked about her daughter, the businesswoman. I could feel the pride in her voice as we discussed the meeting.

I received my MBA in June 1989. As I looked forward to my graduation, I looked back over my life. Thirty years had passed since our fight for an education. My life read like a soap opera. There were valleys so low and hills so high but I had survived. The motto at my elementary school was, "You can make it if you try." I wanted to shout out from the highest hilltop, you can make it if you try. I went down in the field where my Daddy stood and cried out to God when he lost his land. I yelled as loud as I could, "You can make it if you try." I stood bowing as if I was receiving the Grammy Awards. I imagined opening my note and reading my speech, "Thank you God for taking this journey with me. Thank you Grandma Ella for being there with me in my hour of need. Thank you Daddy for your dream of equality and justice. Thank you Momma for love and tenderness to melt away hate. Thank you Andrew for allowing me an opportunity to fall and for being there to pick me up. Bettina, Renée, Erika and Tony, thank you for your patience and love; always aspire to do great things. Counselors, teachers, employers, supervisors and everyone who was a part of my story, thank you." I sat on the ground in the grass and decided that I should write my story.

Andrew built me an office. I bought a computer and the "Writer's Guide". Every time I sat in front of the computer to write, I could not do it. I went to Germany for my son's wedding. While I was in Germany, I went to Italy, France, Spain and Switzerland. I told myself that experiencing life would inspire me to write. It was a wonderful month, however I realized that I was not strong enough to write my story at this point in my life.

I was looking for a company that wanted me for my skills. I started my career over at Atlantic Coast Airline as a Warranty and Rotable Purchasing Agent. I had strong purchasing skills but no airline experience. I read everything I got my hands on about the airline industry. When my suppliers called on me, I asked lots of questions. I had them bring parts and describe how they worked.

It was hard starting over. I had to adjust mentally to an entry-level position. Not having or not being high enough in rank to qualify for business cards was a big deal. Being an individual contributor rather than a manager was also a big deal. The adjustment was made easier because I had a wonderful supervisor, Cheryl Kossman. Our backgrounds were similar; we both had MBAs, purchasing background and similar management styles. She gave me wings and let me fly, her only stipulation was to keep her informed. She fulfilled my every expectation as a supervisor. When I had an opportunity to move back into management with another company, Cheryl was encouraging and supportive.

Cheryl played a major role in my getting on with American Eagle where I experienced another excellent supervisor, George Montoya. Working for George was another wonderful experience. Our backgrounds were similar in as much as George was also a minority. Like Dallas, one of my supervisors at Rubbermaid, George was a strong proponent of the team concept. George and I worked well together because we had different skills and George knew how to capitalize on those differences. George had twenty-five years of airline experience and he was willing to develop my skills by sharing his expertise. Cheryl and George showed me that I had made the right decision to experience another organization.

Where I had to fight for a job announcement system at Rubbermaid, I merely had to learn how to use the system at the airline. Most regional airline employees aspired to work for a major airline and I was no different. American Eagle and American Airlines had one job announcement and bid system that broadcast job opportunities across the system and that boiled down to opportunities beyond my expectations. On the surface, this was the company of my dreams. After two years with American Eagle, I bid on a number of vacancies and had lots of interviews before I landed a position with the major airline, American.

I volunteered to work at the airport to improve my networking base and to expand my knowledge of airport operations. I joined one of the company's resource groups and became chairperson of the Professional

Development Committee. After five years with the company, I finally landed a job at executive level management. At last I was back at the level that I was when I left Rubbermaid.

Under my leadership, the Professional Development Committee developed a mentoring program. We had seventy-five mentoring/protégé relationships involving individuals from the lowest level of the organization to corporate officers. The group's sponsoring officer agreed to be my mentor and to work with me on the project. We had corporate officers at our quarterly meetings sharing dinner with the group. The participants were constantly amazed over the opportunity to relax over dinner with a corporate officer. For so long, I had dreamed that the solution to our racial and economic problems was in our ability to develop a relationship with hiring managers, so that as opportunities arise hiring managers would automatically think of the minority as did Bill Walthers when he chose Don Strosnider for the opportunity in Scheduling. We had one case where a young lady had an opportunity to have dinner with a corporate officer. During the conversation she happened to mention that she had interviewed in a certain department with a certain manager. The officer knew the hiring manager. He learned a little bit about the young lady's credentials and he was impressed. He made a call and the young lady went from being a so-so candidate to we have to have her. Needless to say, she got the job. We had successes but the company needed to do more.

The company's African-American Resource Group scheduled a meeting with the CEO and the Executive Level African-American employees to express concerns and assistance in getting African-Americans in the pipeline for officer candidates. I was one of three individuals who were most vocal in asking questions and offering solutions. One of the suggestions was to hire a VP of Diversity that reported to the CEO. Months passed and the group did not follow-up.

I joined a group who were working with an outside consultant to prepare members of the group to move to the next level. We all shared the cost of this consultant. Most of us worked for the same airline. One of our assignments was to define our passion. I wanted to be this airline's first VP of Diversity. I was inspired to pursue my passion. I started working on a business case for the VP of Diversity.

My mentor reviewed the plan and made suggestions. He also suggested that I let the Resource Group present the business case. Two months later, I had no feedback from the Resource Group and no one was doing anything with the business plan. In the past, I worked alone. I had no patience with people or a group that could not keep moving on a project. I sent an email to the president of the group and asked, "Are you going to do anything with the business plan? If so, when? If not I will do it myself." The approach must have been too aggressive. I contacted the CEO, made an appointment and made the presentation. I had the consultant review my presentation prior to my meeting with the CEO. The CEO told me that the presentation was right on time and that he would be meeting with his team that weekend.

In the meantime, the supervisor that hired me into my executive level management position retired. His replacement reminded me of Craig Sullivan. There were rumors that she drove an African-American employee in her group into a fit of rage and that he was paid to leave the company. I pushed this information to the back of my mind. I made it to this level in my career because I trust when my heart said I could trust. We never developed that level of trust.

I made several unsuccessful attempts to talk to my new supervisor about my career plans to no avail. Then she announced in our staff meeting that she would not be making any nominations for promotions until she could better evaluate our skills. I did not say anything in our staff meeting but I cornered her in her office after the staff meeting. I told her that the closing date was the day before her staff meeting and that I had already submitted my request after being unsuccessful in my attempts to talk to her. I asked that she review my resume and my last performance appraisal and decide if she was able to support my nomination for the vacancy. She asked me to send her an e-mail stating why I felt that I was qualified for the position and she would consider signing the nomination form. She signed the nomination form and I interviewed for both positions. One of the positions would have been a stepping-stone; the other was a dream job. I didn't get either job. I got a "Dear John" letter from the stepping-stone job and a call from the hiring manager of the dream job. The hiring manager of the dream job told me that I came in a close second to the person he hired and that he definitely wanted me on his team.

In another staff meeting, my supervisor shared a copy of the "Human Resource (HR) Leadership Model." The company did, in fact, create a position, "VP Diversity and Talent Management." However, the position reported to the Senior VP of Human Resources whose title changed to Senior VP of Global HR. I wasted no time in contacting the Senior VP of HR asked for an appointment; the CEO shared the diversity business plan with her. We talked about her (HR) Leadership Model. I asked to interview for the VP of Diversity and Talent Management. When I was on vacation in Puerto Vallarta, my secretary called to tell me that the consulting firm that was interviewing the candidates for the VP of Diversity and Talent Management had called to set up an interview. We reviewed my calendar and my secretary called the consultant and set up the interview.

I got a makeover and bought a new suit. I informed my supervisor of the interview. I solicited recommendations from my VP and several other VPs. I put together a "Leadership Profile" presenting supporting documents of my accomplishments. During the interview, I answered every question without hesitation. I thought the interview was going well, I was relaxed and I was having fun. When the consultant finished asking the questions, he said, "There is no doubt that you can do this job but my direction is to go out and find someone who has already developed the best practices. I asked, "In that the case why am I here?" Before I gave him a chance to respond, I thanked him for his time and the interview was over. When I got back to the office, I sent an e-mail to my mentor saying, "The interview was like a roller coaster ride at Six Flags. I was at an all-time high when I thought I was doing good, until the consultant told me that there was no doubt that I could, and would, do a good job; however the roller coaster made a sudden drop when the consultant said that his direction was to go out and find someone who had already developed the best practices. I wondered why I was there. The consultant asked for my mail drop number and I couldn't remember the mail drop number after using it for the past two years. I went out and had a Dairy Queen dipped cone. I have recovered."

Two weeks later, I interviewed for Manager of Diversity. A month later I was laid off.

Chapter 6

The Third Child

*Just as I wondered why I was so much different from the rest of
my siblings, I grew to wonder why my third child was so
much different from her siblings.*

Throughout my life, I have always wondered why I was so different from
the rest of my siblings. In searching my brain I began to realize that
my personality was more like my Father's personality than my Mother's.
Besides it was my Mother who was always saying that you are just like your
Father. As I observed my Father, I realized that there were certain traits that
we had in common. As my children were growing up, I began to observe
certain personality traits in my children. I found some commonality in my
Father, my third child and me. Over and over again, my Mother used one
word to describe my Father and me. I found myself using that same word
over and over again to describe my third child. We were all described as,
DETERMINED!

My Father arrived in his family with a browner complexion than his two
older brothers making him different. His oldest brother was taken to live
in the big house with the white folks and that confused him. His second
brother was sent to live with his maternal grandparents leaving my Father as
basically the oldest child. Then, why are we so much alike?

I arrived into a ready-made family with pre-formed complex relationships. The characteristic that made me different was that I was a girl, however, it wasn't long before my sister arrived on the scene taking away my
unique characteristic.

My third child arrived into a family of girls. The only element that
separated her from her sisters was four years. Just as I wondered why I was
so much different from the rest of my siblings, I grew to wonder why my
third child was so much different from her siblings. My daughter was the
apple of her father's eye. They both had the same crooked baby finger;

the same eye stigma and they were both diabetics. We both shared the fact that we were more like our fathers but our common thread was our DETERMINATION.

Erika wanted to come in first in a beauty pageant. She participated in so many pageants. We tried to explain that beauty pageants had nothing to do with beauty; they were predictable. First place was always given to a white girl, second place was always a colored girl and it always came down to Erika or Missy Jackson. We knew it, it happened all the time. During the two years of pageantry, she received four first runner-up trophies and one second-place trophy. It was heart breaking, watching her going through this routine time after time. She finally stopped focusing on the beauty pageants.

She tried out for cheerleading four years in a row. The first year she became a diabetic. During the course of that summer, she went from seventy pounds to one hundred and four pounds. When she tried out for cheerleading she was considered fat. She practiced so hard to master the split. She mastered the split but she didn't make the team. The kids in school made fun of her. Her brother got one of his worst whippings when I heard him call her "fatso."

In September, on or about that same time her father was diagnosed as a diabetic. I changed the way I cooked and Erika began to lose weight almost as fast as she gained the weight. It was crazy. She was only thirteen but I thought Erika was using drugs. She would get sick and by the time the doctor's appointment rolled around she was all right. During the night she tiptoed back and forth to the kitchen drinking punch or water. When I finally got her in to see the doctor, her sugar was six hundred and she was down to fifty pounds. She was taken from the doctor's office to the hospital.

The doctor put Erika on a sugar-free diet. As when I was in the hospital, you could ask for stuff and get almost anything you want within reason. Erika wanted pickles and the doctor said it was all right; therefore, I bought her a jar of pickles. Having a large family, it was only natural to get a large jar of pickles. Erika ate all of the pickles in the jar in one day. The doctor discovered that the diet was too low in calories. She was put on a twenty-six-hundred calorie diet and had to have snacks in between meals. If she missed meals or her snacks she would faint.

Erika was the first of our children to have any type of major illness. The whole family had to go to classes to learn about diabetes. We all had to learn to give Erika her shots. I did fine giving the orange a shot but when it came time to actually giving Erika a shot, I shook so bad I couldn't do it. After Erika got out of the hospital, we had to take Erika for her blood work in the mornings before she had breakfast. I would take her to the appointment, and then take her to Andrew's job for Andrew to give her the shot. We could no longer simply give her a breakfast sandwich at fast food establishment; we had to take her to a restaurant to have a balanced diet.

Erika rejected the idea of being a diabetic. She perceived that it made her different. She rejected the idea of being different. She would not eat her snacks in between meals because it meant that she had to eat in class in front of the other kids who were not allowed to eat. She was also afraid of getting fat again. She would not wear her medical identification bracelet or necklace that identified her as a diabetic. I tried negotiating but nothing worked. I was often pushed into keeping her home from the pool while the other children went to the pool because she refused to wear the medical identification.

After four times of trying out for cheerleading she finally made the team. When my Mother use to say that I was so determined, I perceived that being determined was a negative thing until I saw how many times that Erika kept doing things until she finally made it. I was proud of her and I had to admire her determination. The accomplishments from her determination were negated by her stubbornness. Along with being a cheerleader came responsibility. We encouraged all of our children to participate in extra-curriculum activities and we made them take responsibility for doing their homework and making good grades. When her first report card came in with bad grades, we talked to her teachers. We found that Erika wasn't doing her homework. We worked with Erika to get her homework done. The second report card came with no improvement. She wasn't turning in the homework. We had to get to the threats. We told Erika, "If there are no improvements in your grades by the next report card, you have to quit cheer-leading." It broke my heart having to make her quit cheerleading but she left me with no choice.

During the summer, we did not allow the children to watch a lot of TV. We used to play a game to generate conversation and to find out what the children were doing. We played "truth and NO consequences." The children loved confessing to things they got away with. By the time Erika and Tony came along they had to be quite creative in getting away with mischief.

We had a rule in the family that the all the children could not go out on a date with the opposite sex until they were sixteen. It was a rule that we were determined to keep. If it was left to my husband, he would have been like my father and I couldn't let that happened to my children. I didn't want my son to be treated any different from my girls because I knew how I felt when my brothers were given opportunities that I was not given.

Erika climbed out the window to go out. We thought we had a peeping tom only to find out that Erika had been climbing out the window. Erika got a kick out of thinking that she had gotten away with sneaking out. She confessed during "truth and NO consequences."

When Erika graduated from high school, she decided to go to nursing school. She was working part time in the hospital. She hadn't been on the job three weeks when she came home and told us that she had to dress down a dead person. She acted as though it didn't bother her. I had already determined that it took a special person to be a nurse because that is the one profession that is beyond my ability. One day out of the blue she quit nursing school and quit her job. She told us that it was just too sad.

For weeks she moped around the house sleeping all day and out all night until two and three in the morning. I could not help but to reflect back on the turmoil in my life just after I finished high school. During one of our arguments, I echoed my Father's words, "For as long as you live in my house you will live by my rules." And there it was my past staring me in the face haunting me as I was trying to deal with my daughter's problems. In a moment of despair, I called Tommy, Erika's fiancé. He told me that Erika was upset because he was doing drugs. The $5,000 that they had saved for when they got married was gone up in smoke. When I approached Erika about my conversation with Tommy she got angry. I wished the children had come with some instructions because we didn't know what to do.

My sister had a Masters in Psychology. I called her for advice. She suggested that I get Erika away from the drugs as soon as possible. We packed up Erika and she moved to D.C. to live with her sister. My sister got Erika a job working at the school where my sister was the principal. Andrew saw Tommy driving around town with another girl. We did not mention this to Erika but she found out. Not only was Tommy two-timing Erika; but the other girl was pregnant by Tommy.

One day one of the girls from human resources came to my desk. She was processing insurance claims and there was a claim for Erika, for a miscarriage. She said, "We are friends and I know enough about you and your family to suspect that you are not aware of this. I can't process a claim for anything dealing with a pregnancy for one of your dependents." I sat at my desk trying to compose myself. I thanked my friend for bringing this situation to my attention. Both Andrew and I talked to Erika. We suspected that she got pregnant on purpose.

One day as I was driving through town, I saw Erika's car parked in the driveway at the home of one of her friends. I knocked on the door and Erika answered the door. Erika was as shocked to see me, as I was to see her. I asked, "What's going on? She replied, "This is my life and I am going to live it my way." Erika ended-up moving in with Tommy and getting pregnant again.

Erika was in and out of work. Erika's workplace was robbed and Tommy was a prime suspect. She either quit or she was fired, the fact was that she discontinued her employment at that particular job. Tommy was in and out of jail and rehab. The day my first grandson, Eric, was born; I was there at the hospital. When the lady came in to fill out the birth certificate, I was amazed at how much things had changed. Erika could choose the race of her baby. I asked, "What happened to the three percent colored blood rule?" The girl looked at me as if she thought I was crazy, she was too young to understand. In the old days, if you had three percent colored blood, your race was colored. No ifs, ands, or buts about it. I wanted to put American rather than black or white. Erika ended-up putting Eric's race as African-American. She could not give the baby Tommy's last name during the initial paperwork for his birth certificate. Despite our concerns, Erika and Tommy went to Richmond and had Eric's name changed to Jones.

Tommy was found guilty of eighteen felonies and given a twenty-year suspended sentence contingent upon participating in the Community Diversion Incentive Program and he had to make restitution of $8,489 in payments of $100. They lived together for about two years and they never married. When Erika left Tommy taking Eric, I took care of Eric while Erika worked. I took him home to visit with his mother on her days off. Eric and I became so attached that he cried when I took him back to visit with his mother. When Eric was five, I knew that I had to get out of the picture and let Eric and his mother bond. Eric went to live with his mom full time and went to day care.

While in day care, Eric picked up the usual germs and was sick quite often. Erika, being a diabetic picked-up the germs, too. Erika lost her job because of absenteeism. She ended-up applying for assistance. Tommy was ordered to pay child support. Tough times don't last forever and Erika had my fighting spirit. She got a job at Media General Cable. She loved the job and she was good at it. She constantly received awards for top sales. She was a natural in sales.

Life was good. My Dad had retired from the Viscose, sold more than half of the farmland and retired from farming. He was having a good time living his dream; providing assistance to and building homes for low- and moderate-income families. Erika had her dream job. I had my dream job with the airline, Eric was in school in the first grade, there was peace in all of our lives. Three generations of the third child at peace.

Erika thought she was in love again. Her fiancé got a job in Lake City, Florida. He asked Erika to marry him and move with him to Florida. Erika quit her job, they got married and moved to Florida. Lake City was a small town that did not provide many job opportunities or affordable childcare providers for before and after school care. It wasn't long before Erika hooked-up with the wrong crowd and got involved with drugs.

When Erika's husband called and told us that she had been arrested, I dropped everything and flew to her rescue. I posted her bond and got her out of jail. She was arrested for possession of stolen property. Erika told me that her girlfriend gave her the ring to pawn because she had better negotiating skills and that she didn't know the ring was stolen. I had no reason not to believe her.

A couple of months later, I got another call from her husband. He had hesitated in calling me but he was at the end of his rope. He gave Erika $1,800 to pay for a package that required cash on delivery. Erika took the money and disappeared. She had been gone five days when he called. He gave me the details of her addiction. She had disappeared before but never longer than three or four days. I had just started a new position and I didn't really want to take the time off from work. We called our son, Tony, who was more street-wise than my husband or me. My husband and our son went to Florida to see what they could do. In the meantime, I called the bail bondsman and he informed me that we could have her bond revoked and she could be put back in jail.

Of all the people in the world, Erika called Tommy. Tony and Tommy were friends since high school. Tommy called Tony and they were able to find her. When she returned home the bail bondsman was there with the police to take her to jail. Eric was sent to the neighbors. The police carried her from the house kicking and screaming all kinds of obscenities. When it was all over, my husband called me. He was so drained and broken. He said, "When it was all over, they sat in the living room in silence." He said, "I can't understand what went wrong."

Erika called me from jail uttering the same obscenities. She said that I had neglected her as a child, she had been raped, nobody knew or cared and that it was my fault because I was so busy in school. I had blamed my parents when I was so miserable after I graduated from high school. I had not told a living soul about my rape. Therefore, it was easy for me to accept the blame for her troubles. Tony took Eric back to Virginia. Tommy moved swiftly to move Eric in with him. By this time he was seven thousand dollars in arrearage on his child support.

My heart was broken. I could cry uncontrollably for hours. I cried on the way to work. I went to the car at lunchtime and cried during lunch. I cried on my way home from work. I cried myself to sleep at night. My eyes were red and my face was puffy. I told people that it was my sinuses causing the red eyes and puffy face. My boss asked if everything was all right. I shook my head yes and rushed away before he could see the tears. I was blessed to have a kind, gentle and patient boss, Tom Merold. I went back to my desk and sent him an e-mail telling him what was going on. I asked that he not push me to talk because, I couldn't. I could answer any questions by e-mail. That's how we communicated over this subject matter. I worked odd hours to minimize my contact with people. Sometimes I was in the office at four in the morning. When I couldn't sleep, I went to work. I purchased my personal laptop and Tom helped me to link to my workstation so that I could keep-up my excellent performance.

One evening Tom was coming in from a meeting as I was leaving at two in the afternoon. The tears flowed down my face, he hugged me and I wept uncontrollably. Neither one of us uttered a word. He embraced me until my crying subsided. He sent me an e-mail saying that he felt so helpless and asked if there was anything that he could do. I wrote back from home saying, "Thank you for your patience, understanding and for allowing my flexible schedule. Continue to pray for me and my family."

We had been in Texas less than six months and we were looking for a church home. I was looking for a predominately African-American, medium-size Baptist church. One of my friends came to visit from Nashville. She wanted us to go to the Potter's House. Andrew and I talked about joining

St. Michael Baptist Church that Sunday but we put off our plans to go to the Potter's House with our friends. When we got to the church we had to wait in this long line to get in the parking lot. I started to fuss because the last thing I was looking for was a big church like this one and a TV minister. Gwethlyn was Pentecostal and Momma use to say those people were crazy. They spoke in tongues and they ran all over the church like crazy people. I was so deep in trouble; I didn't have time to be fooling with this mess. We finally got in the church and got situated.

We were among friends, but they didn't know what I was going through. I tried to fight back the tears. Once the tears started to fall, I tried not to wipe them so that no one would notice that I was crying. One of the ushers handed me some tissues. The front of my dress was wet as if I had been sprayed with a water gun. I took a hand-full of tissues. Bishop Jakes' sermon was titled, "Help." The Bishop screamed, "Help!" I had no control. I screamed, "Help!" I could not stop screaming, "Help, help, help." He said, "The devil is a liar. Don't let the devil have your daughter. March up in that crack house and say, devil, you can't have my daughter! Take back what the devil stole from you." I don't even remember getting up out of my seat, but the next thing I knew, I was laying on the alter and I looked over there was my friend Traice. I forgot about where I was and I asked Traice, "What are you doing up here?" Traice began to testify about what was going on with her son and I told her about my daughter. We cried, we hugged and we prayed together. We both joined that crazy church.

At first, I could not tell my parents that I joined that crazy church. I kept telling myself that I would stay long enough to get healed and move my membership to a more conventional Baptist church. It was almost as if the Bishop heard me thinking. He said, "Don't deny your blessing." I went back to that crazy church the following Wednesday night for Bible study. I couldn't wait for Sunday and Wednesday. I stopped crying and became a crazy praying person. I started sending Erika tapes and telling her, "The devil can't have you." When I told my parents that I had joined the Potters House and that Bishop Jakes was my pastor. I had a story on spiritual healing.

I had not been as close to God since I was eighteen-years-old and in so much trouble with my spirit. It was easy to have faith when the problems were small but when it came to my child and having to have her put in jail and fighting demonic forces like crack, it took crazy faith. I told Momma, "You were right, those people are crazy and I had to become just as crazy as they are to keep from losing my mind." My Momma sweetly and innocently said, "How do you consult with your pastor?" I said, "Momma, every Sunday and every Wednesday night my pastor counsels thousands of us at one time. He taught me how to pray for myself and yes, I can lay hands on myself." I grew-up thinking that I had to talk face-to-face with Rev. Frank to figure out how to make it through the day. Being a kid, I probably needed that. There were times when I called the prayer line when I needed that extra measure of faith.

Erika stayed in jail for seventy-seven days. She entered a guilty plea to "dealing in stolen property." She got ninety days in jail with credit for time served, Drug Offender Probation, drug evaluation and treatment including urinalysis, one hundred hours community service work and she had to make restitution of two-hundred-and-fifty dollars.

As soon as Erika got out of jail, we flew to Virginia to get Eric. Tommy had filed for custody in Virginia. Eric had held up like a trooper. The day that Tommy refused to let Eric go with us was one of the hardest days of our life. Eric cried so hard that my heart broke. I told Eric that we had to go to court but I promised that he would be back with his mother. I called in to take a day of vacation. We stayed over until that Monday to secure a lawyer. I took more vacation to go to court with Erika. The court determined that Florida had jurisdiction in the case. I had to take more vacation to secure a lawyer in Florida. When we went to court in Florida, Tommy and Erika were given joint custody and Erika was named the custodial parent.

It seemed that the harder she tried the more difficult the situation became. Erika's husband lost his car and got behind in his bills because of the number of bad checks she had written when she was using drugs. I paid for the travel expenses and the legal fees.

I was flabbergasted when I learned the details of Drug Offender Probation. In my opinion it was house arrest. Erika had to visit with her probation officer once a week and randomly submit to a drug test. He reminded me of the white overseers that were so familiar in the slave movies. He constantly threatened to violate her probation when she got behind in paying for her counseling, restitution or payments to the Department of Correction. When I took a closer look at the plea agreement, I realized the court system and her public defender had screwed Erika. I asked our paid attorney to look into the violation of probation. He wrote a letter to Erika's probation officer asking that he be contacted when the warrant was issued so that he could see to turning her in and having an appropriate bond set.

I took a week of vacation and went to Florida. I spoke face-to-face with her Probation Officer (Kevin). He gave me a print-out of the cost and how much it would cost to keep Erika out of jail. Her drug treatment consisted of counseling that cost over a thousand dollars that had to be paid to the Salvation Army Correctional Services. I paid seven-hundred-and-sixty-two dollars and thirty-nine cents to the Salvation Army.

I couldn't determine the bottom line amount that she owed to the State of Florida Department of Corrections Court, but I paid eight-hundred-and-forty-six dollars and ninety-six cents of that cost. I paid another one-hundred-and-twelve dollars to "Tri-County for Susan." I don't know what it was for, all I knew was that to save my grandchild, I had to save his mother.

Our next order of business was to help Erika get a job. She got a job at a restaurant as a waitress about three blocks from where she lived. Almost every other weekend, we flew to the Jacksonville airport, rented a car and usually arrived at Erika's house around one or two in the morning on Saturday, to make sure Eric and Erika were all right. We left on Sunday around midday. It was a hard and expensive journey. Eric got out of school for summer vacation and Erika sent him to me for summer vacation. Erika had a month left on her Drug Offender's Probation.

One week before Erika was suppose to complete her Drug Offender Probation, she went off with a girl from work, used crack, failed her drug test and was sent back to jail. She spent six more months in jail.

Within a week, Tommy was granted custodial parent of Eric. In a last ditch effort, I refused to send Eric home to Virginia until Tommy paid for the airline ticket. Tommy did not send the money for the airline ticket until the week before Labor Day. Eric stayed with me all summer. We went to Six Flags almost every evening and he played at the pool almost every day. I knew that our relationship would change forever.

I believed that I had failed my child and my grandchild until I learned from one of Bishop's sermons that the battle was not mine to fight. Hopeless to do anything about Erika or Eric's situation, I surrendered my will to do God's will. I sat in my private place and said, "Lord, I surrender! Whatever it is that you want me to do show me the way." He restored my spirit. I was persecuted but not forsaken. I was perplexed but not in despair. Trouble was all around me. I grew weary but God gave me the strength. I could sing when I felt like weeping. I could hang in there when I felt like giving up. I could be calm when I felt like fighting. In the midst of the storm, I knew that He was with me.

Erika's marriage fell apart. I continued to visit her in jail. It was so hard to keep the faith. The jail officials would send Erika home on weekends. She had no transportation. I could not send cab fare money, therefore I had to call a taxi from Texas, and pay with my credit card to get her back and forth. When she needed medical supplies, she took the taxi to Wal-Mart, gathered up medical supplies and personal items. When the items were tallied, the check-out attendant called me, verified that the person in the check-out line was Erika, called off the items being purchased and the total charges. Sometimes the process went smoothly, other times it turned into a nightmare.

On one occasion, I received a call informing me that I had to go to a Wal-Mart here in Texas, show my credit card and ID. I had made lunch plans with one of my co-workers. I told her that I had to make a quick stop at Wal-Mart. At two-thirty that afternoon, I called back to the office to say that I had some problems during lunch and since Stacie was having lunch with me, she too was detained. I couldn't explain to Stacie why making this transaction was so important and why it was so complicated without sounding crazy. Finally, I simply told her the truth. One of the reasons I hated telling anyone about my problems was because they usually didn't know what to say and there really weren't any words of comfort or they would say I'm so sorry. Those words made me feel as though I was sorry for being in this situation.

Erika finally got out of jail, divorced her husband and moved in with a recovering alcoholic because, "he understood her problems." We had some peace of mind for about six months. Just when you expect things to get better, they get worse. Erika had some medical problems and the doctors told her that she would never be able to have any more children. Well, Erika got pregnant.

My Daddy got sick. The family gathered in Virginia to visit my Dad. I sent my credit card to Erika so that she could rent a car, pay for a hotel along the way and put gas in the car. She made the trip and returned home to Florida without any problems. Before I could get my credit card back Erika fell off the wagon and disappeared. By the time I cancelled my credit card I was seventeen hundred dollars further in debt. I was cast down but I was not destroyed.

By the time her second child, Derrick, was born, I was simply praying that he would be healthy. He was alright. Before her son was a year old she was pregnant again. The children's father got in trouble with the law and went to jail.

At last my prayers were answered. Erika agreed to move to Texas. I flew to Florida, rented a one-way moving truck. We packed her things in the truck and Erika, Derrick and I drove straight through only stopping for rest breaks and meals.

I had the good sense to know that we could never live together. I rented an apartment for Erika and the kids. Trying to support two households stretched our finances almost to the breaking point. We were in a period of austerity. With every purchasing decision, we looked at the item and made a decision based on want or need. If it didn't pass the need test, we didn't buy it.

Within two months of coming to Texas Erika had a job. She could only work part-time because she was pregnant. I was so proud of her as she step-by-step became the number one sales person. She got toxemia and went into labor during her sixth month of pregnancy. The beautiful baby girl came into this world weighing only three and a half pounds. Erika named her Gabriel. She looked like a doll baby. She was only fourteen inches long. My best girlfriend, Elsa, bought a doll outfit for Gabriel to wear home from the hospital. Erika got out of the hospital after seven days, however, Gabriel stayed in the hospital for five weeks. At one point Gabriel forgot to breathe and we all had to learn how to take CPR training on an infant. When it was time for Erika to go back to work, Andrew took care of Gabriel because we didn't want to expose her to the world. Derrick went to day care. In ten months Erika was able to pay her rent and take care of her bills.

Chapter 7

On the Wings of the Past

*My struggles didn't extinguish my self-respect, crush my ambition
or paralyze my efforts to pursue my dreams.*

President Abraham Lincoln issued the Emancipation Proclamation on January 1, 1863. The proclamation gave slaves their freedom and is considered an important benchmark in the African-American struggle for freedom and equality. Because it had been a crime for slaves to learn to read or write, many former slaves had no way of knowing that they were free. Many former slaves had never been off the farms, nor did they have any idea of how to take care of themselves or their families. When the proclamation was issued, it really did not free all of the slaves since the Confederate states did not recognize President Lincoln's authority. In Texas, though technically freed in 1863, according to southern folklore the slaves did not learn of their freedom until the arrival of the Union soldiers on June 19, 1865, two-and-one-half years after the proclamation was first issued. It was not until after the Civil War that the 13th Amendment to the United States Constitution, ratified in 1865 officially outlawed slavery.

Many Southern African-Americans celebrate "Juneteenth." The word June-teenth comes from the words June and 19th. Juneteenth should serve as a valuable lesson on the importance and value of education and the realization that slave labor was vital to the economic prosperity of our nation.

During the time that I was researching oral history for my book "*Freedom Road,*" I interviewed an older woman. After two hours of being offered everything to eat from sandwiches to cake and reviewing every picture in the house she began to talk. In the middle of the family Bible was a tattered and torn piece of paper. She gently opened the old fragile note. It was her great grandfather's note that identified him as a free man. It had survived over one hundred years tucked away in the Bible because too many people believed that the history of slavery should be forgotten. Tears rolled down her cheeks as she talked about the stories that she had heard as a child about her family. Her great grandfather was a free colored man but her great grandmother was a slave and all their children were slaves. She said that when slavery ended their master called them in and said they were free. He could not afford to pay them or keep them on the farm. There were no forty acres and a mule. Like many of the former slaves, her family had never been off the farm. They were given two days rations of food and sent on their way. Her stories left an impression on my life. When I went through my crying times, I thought about the challenges of my ancestors and I drew strength and courage from them. They endured and persevered with determination, courage, faith, hope and prayers.

I often wondered what happened to the slave children who were separated from their parents during slavery! I found in my research for "*Freedom Road*" the "Register of Colored Persons Cohabitating Together" along with the corresponding Virginia Law. Title 30, Chapter C111, of the Code of Virginia Act passed 1865: WHEN COLORED PERSONS NOT MARRIED SHALL BE DEEMED TO BE HUSBAND AND WIFE; THEIR CHILDREN SHALL BE LEGITIMATED, "where colored persons before the passage of this act shall have undertaken and agreed to occupy the relation of each other of husband and wife, and shall be cohabitating together as such at the time of its passage, whether the rites of marriage have been solemnized between them or not, they shall be deemed husband and wife and be entitled to the rights and privileges, and subject to the duties and obligations of that relation in like manner as if they had been duly married by law; and all their children shall be deemed legitimate." When I saw strange families on the Cohabitation List, a couple far too young to have ten children, I asked the older woman, "Where did the children whose parents were sold to other farms go when slavery ended?" She said that they were a slave family on the farm and they remained a part of the slave family when slavery ended. I could see how the community lifestyle that I experienced as a child had evolved. The lesson was that we all have a responsibility in helping one another especially the children.

Slavery ended but the persistent denial of rights and subjection to humiliating indignities continued. The "separate but equal" doctrine established in the case of *Plessy v. Ferguson* (1896) constitutionalized discrimination and sanctioned segregation. It was not until after World War II that Negroes began to advance in education, social status and leadership and was able to fight at the federal-level to achieve a major victory in *Brown v. Board of Education of Topeka* (1954). In winning this case the court stated, "in the field of public education the doctrine of 'separate but equal' has no place . . . Separate educational facilities are inherently not equal." The war was on. Now my learning moves closer to home.

It was no longer my ancestors exhibiting great strength, courage, endurance, perseverance, determination, faith, moving forward with hope and prayers. It was my Daddy, Charlie Dean, Sam Fletcher, young men and women from my community. They were ordinary people with very little formal education working menial jobs. I was too young to understand the full impact of their dream, but I knew that bullets fired at the house couldn't stop them. Cross burning in the yard couldn't stop them. Bloody sheet on the mailbox couldn't stop them. Mutilation of the livestock couldn't stop them. No form of intimidation or threats on their lives could stop them. They collectively dreamed of economic prosperity for their children and that dream was shatterproof.

I noticed that there was a group of people outside my immediate community exhibiting great strength, courage, endurance, perseverance, determination and faith, moving forward with hope and prayers. This man called Martin Luther King Jr. was as unstoppable as my Daddy and our leaders from Happy Creek. When he delivered his famous "I have a dream" speech at the 100 anniversary of the Emancipation Proclamation, I was old enough to understand. He verbalized the dream that Daddy had tried to instill in us during integration.

Under the leadership of Dr. King, and with the blood of numerous Civil Rights activists, African-Americans marched, protested and gave their lives in a struggle for our rights under the constitution. President Lyndon Johnson signed the Civil Rights Act on July 2, 1964. It guaranteed that "No person in the United States shall, on the ground of race, color, or national origin, be excluded from participation in, be denied the benefits of, or subject to discrimination."

All this time God was preparing me. The time had come for me to pick up my cross and go forth. I believed that I had paid my dues and then some. I fought having to step forth and fight discrimination on the job. Dr. King gave his life for the cause. When I wanted to die, God wouldn't take me. I know! I wanted to give up not die for the cause. God knew too.

I had to learn that when God gives you a job to do, it is easier to simply say, "Yes Lord, yes Lord." He had allowed me to become educated. He had entered into some battles with me and we won. I took the credit and acted as though I had made all of the accomplishments myself.

Then He brought me to my knees. It was there in the midst of the storm, that I finally threw up my hands and surrendered to His will. My struggles didn't extinguish my self-respect, crush my ambition or paralyze my efforts to pursue my dreams. It was the struggles that gave me the will to achieve my dreams and to find God's purpose in my life. His Word, Romans 5:3-5 . . . There is glory in tribulations knowing that tribulations worketh patience; and patience, experience; and experience, hope; and hope maketh not ashamed; . . .

It was in Him and His Word that I discovered the extraordinary power within. He equipped me with the same characteristics of my ancestors, my father, our Happy Creek community leaders and Dr. King; strength, courage, endurance, perseverance, determination, faith and hope. These traits had been there inside of me all my life. He simply had to bring me to a place where I could hear His Word. That same power is in each of us, all we have to do is submit our will to His.